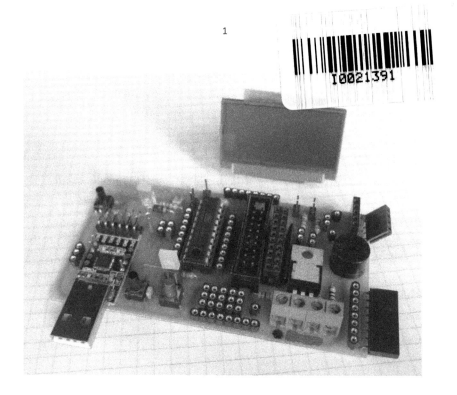

The ATTINY Project

Why FORTH?

Combined English and German Version
Georg Heinrichs

Translated into English, edited and published
by Juergen Pintaske, ExMark

The current Forth Bookshelf of eBooks and print books can be found at
https://www.amazon.co.uk/Juergen-Pintaske/e/B00N8HVEZM

1 Charles Moore - Forth - The Early Years: Background information about the beginnings of this Computer Language

2 Charles Moore - Programming A Problem Oriented Language: Forth - how the internals work

3 Leo Brodie - Starting Forth -The Classic

4 Leo Wong – Juergen Pintaske – Stephen Pelc FORTH LITE TUTORIAL: Code tested with free MPE VFX Forth, SwiftForth and Gforth or else

5 Juergen Pintaske – A START WITH FORTH - Bits to Bites Collection – 12 Words to start, then 35 Words, Javascript Forth on the Web, more

6 Stephen Pelc - Programming Forth: Version July 2016

7 Brad Rodriguez - Moving Forth / TTL CPU / B.Y.O. Assembler

8 Tim Hentlass - Real Time Forth

9 Chen-Hanson Ting - Footsteps In An Empty Valley issue 3

10 Chen-Hanson Ting - Zen and the Forth Language: EFORTH for the MSP430G2552 from Texas Instruments

11 Chen-Hanson Ting - eForth and Zen – 3rd Edition 2017: with 32-bit 86eForth v5.2 for Visual Studio 2015

12 Chen-Hanson Ting - eForth Overview

13 Chen-Hanson Ting - FIG-Forth Manual Document /Test in 1802 IP

14 Chen-Hanson Ting - EP32 RISC Processor IP: Description and Implementation into FPGA – ASIC tested by NASA

15 Chen-Hanson Ting - Irriducible Complexity

16 Chen-Hanson Ting - Arduino controlled by eForth

17 Burkhard Kainka - Learning Programming with MyCo: Learning Programming easily - independent of a PC (Forth code to follow soon)

18 Burkhard Kainka - BBC Micro:bit: Tests Tricks Secrets Code, Additional MicroBit information when running the Mecrisp Package

19 Burkhard Kainka – Thomas Baum – Web Programming ATYTINY13

20 Georg Heinrichs - The ATTINY 2313 Project – Why Forth?

Contents / Inhalt combined English and German version

http://www.g-heinrichs.de/wordpress/index.php/attiny/

	Software for download:	
	MikroForth-Compiler MikroForth-Vokabular	
	http://www.g-heinrichs.de/wordpress/index.php/attiny/downloads/	

Pictures and Figures:

D pages for the German version

Appendix:

Document MikroForth_v18f_A5 English German

Intentionally left blank

Introduction

2018 is the time to celebrate **50 Years of Forth.**
This year in September is as well **EuroForth 2018** – where the Forth specialists meet

-     this time **at the river of Forth in Scotland**
-     and **the inventor of Forth – Chuck Moore**, has been invited to attend,
-     and he promised he will be there.

I had started the Forth Bookshelf 5 years ago, and it has now – including this book – grown to 20 books altogether.

First to be published as eBook for cost reasons and no delivery cost.
But many people want to hold the print book in their hands, so this year I started converting, and the first 6 books are available now as print book as well – with more to come over the next couple of months.

I stumbled by chance over this project of Georg Heinrichs, when I was looking for a Forth for the small Microchip Attiny 2313.

There really is a small Forth implementation with the whole Forth on the chip – but I have not tried it yet.

The 2313 has it's limitations
    with just 2k of Flash.

But on the positive side there is
    a 20 pin DIL-package.

So very breadboard friendly.
Easy PCB to make if needed.
There are smaller packages, if you can deal with it.

But there was another reason for me as well:

There is one other book on the Forth Bookshelf - the Sparrow;

where there is no Forth implementation yet, as it uses the Attiny13, which is even smaller with its 8 pin DIL package – and 1k FLASH.

BUT SPARROW can be programmed over the internet – no PC, no special software, no programmer required, just your mobile phone/PC, and this chip here could be probably used as a target for this MikroForth as well. Still to be tested.

Back to the MikroForth project here now:
I contacted Georg and started with a first translation, as his German version would be a bit difficult to digest for a worldwide audience.
He agreed to the translation.

We started a Wiki page on the German Forth group website, and there is much of this available now for download and print at https://wiki.forth-ev.de/doku.php/attiny

More to be added as there is time.
I do like the approach that Georg took and he kindly agreed that I can convert his information into an eBook –
and later then as well
as print book as part of Forth Bookshelf at https://www.amazon.co.uk/Juergen-Pintaske/e/B00N8HVEZM

Anybody with a 2313 chip, a resistor and a capacitor – plus a USBtoTTL converter can get going as the software runs on the PC and generates a hex-file for programming.

Georg offers as well chips with a Bootloader programmed in already:
You can find his website at
http://www.g-heinrichs.de/wordpress/

A complete kit of parts including the PCB – as shown on the cover page.
And as well a pre-programmed chip 2313 with a bootloader already programmed in.

There is as well a blog in German at
 http://www.forum.g-heinrichs.de/viewforum.php?f=12

But the project can be built using a solderless breadboard as well.
Or some other options I tried out and documented here in additional pages in the appendix.

One of the points important to me is to have a system in a box including batteries, so you can run an application without problems – and in an enclosure which is probably available worldwide – I often use a TicTac Box as we needed a low-cost enclosure for the MicroBox project.

I tried this out to ensure it all works. But just take it as example and find your own way.

Enjoy the Book – the print version planned is now available in 2018/19, there was interest.

I took the decision to make this documentation available as a combined version in English for the non-German world, but to keep as well Georg's original in German – rather than publishing two separate items.

I had been planning to have the eBook available on amazon around EuroForth (12th of September) so there had to be a preliminary version. Updated now.

We hope you enjoy this book, get a chip and try it out
– and please leave a bit of feedback at amazon, so other readers can use your feedback as guidance.

I am often asked why Forth – there is Python, C, and many other languages.
But I like Forth – it seems that it is like Marmite – you like it or you hate it.
As you can see from my work regarding the Forth Bookshelf – I do like Forth.

Enjoy reading.
And if you have access to the necessary hardware – try it out. I did and enjoyed it, which led to this book.

Please comment on amazon to help others with your feedback.
Direct feedback regarding this book please to epldfpga@aol.com

Juergen Pintaske, ExMark, 01 October 2018   2018_09_18fp.

0 How FORTH started

Forth was developed by Charles H. Moore 1969. FORTH has a number of peculiarities, that make it very different from conventional programming languages. FORTH represents i.e. not only a development environment, but also an operating system.
These peculiarities can be easily explained from the history of the origin. Moore had bought a computer without a software to control the telescope of an observatory.
He had planned to program all the components himself, which are necessary for a comfortable programming and operation of the computer. These include an operating system, a language and a development environment. All these components were realized within a single program – the Forth system.

Picture 1: The inventor of Forth Charles H. Moore

Moore later told himself: *I developed FORTH over the course of several years as an interface between me and the computers that I programmed. The traditional languages did not provide the performance, simplicity or flexibility that I wanted. I hated many valid wisdoms to incorporate exactly the skills a productive programmer needs. The most important of these is the possibility to add new properties, which are necessary later.*

*When I first combined the ideas that I had developed into one unit, I worked on an IBM 1130 see **Picture 2**, a computer of the "third generation". The result seemed to me so powerful that I thought of it as a "language of the fourth generation of computers". I would have called it FOURTH, but the 1130 allowed only an identifier with 5 letters.*

So, from FOURTH to FORTH, a nice play on words.

(Cited from L. Brodie: Starting FORTH)

(Forth = forward)

Picture 2 : The IBM 1130, here Forth ran first

Example source: http://computermuseum.informatik.uni-stuttgart.de/dev/ibm1130/ibm1130.html

1 How MikroForth started

One day, my son came to me – he was just 14 years old – and asked me how to make a compiler. He wanted to program one himself.

Now, I had once read about how to build compilers; But that had been many years ago and I had forgotten most of it.

However, I could still very well remember, that compiler construction is somewhat more complex and hardly anything for a 14-year-old. And I told him that.

But he did not let go and kept asking again. A few months later – I was working on the concept of a Microcontroller Training – we came up with the idea of programming a compiler for the Atmel/Microchip ATtiny 2313 microcontroller. As a language to write this compiler for, we chose FORTH, not least because of the simple structure of this language.

Our FORTH compiler should not run on the microcontroller itself, but on a PC: This compiler should convert the FORTH code into machine code, which should then be uploaded to the Attiny.

The compiler itself is rather straightforward: it accesses a database which contains a collection of A-words (command sequences in machine code – and the A stands for Assembler) and F-words (command sequences in FORTH code).

Since we were mainly concerned about the principle, we did not implemented all common FORTH words (commands), but only a small subset.

It was extremely instructive to write such a compiler program, and I can only advise anyone to try it yourself. Micro-FORTH makes this possible; As it is an open system: the database can be changed and expanded as desired. This is exactly the same as Moore's leading concept wanted it.

We were particularly fascinated by the following: when we started the project, we only knew a few of FORTH's essential characteristics. Later, when the project was almost finished, we once researched how a FORTH compilation works in other implementations. And to our surprise – we found some of our ideas in there to be exactly ythe same.

What can you get out of looking at FORTH:
- Understanding simple Compilers
- Understanding of Assembler and Machine Code
- Understanding and practice of handling Stacks
- Understanding how to pass Parameters
- Last – but not least: how to write efficient Machine Code

2 Getting into MikroForth

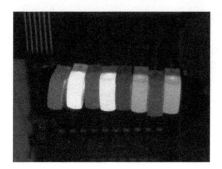

Picture 3: The 8 LED Display example

MikroForth is a FORTH compiler for the ATtiny 2313. This means: The program is entered on a PC and then compiled. The generated HEX code is then transferred into the Attiny with a Flash Programming utility.

In a step-by-step procedure, we will show you how to deal with MikroForth in this chapter. For this purpose, we will first program the ATtiny with MikroForth program to generate an LED pattern on Port B as shown in **Picture 3**.

We will simply specify the few FORTH language elements required first; how they work, - and above all - how to develop own programs, we will explain in the following chapters.

Let's start with the installation of MikroForth:
Just copy the Forth directory into the program directory (or another directory of your choice).
Or let us assume you start a new Folder c:/microforth. Then
Download the software from http://www.g-heinrichs.de/attiny/forth/forth2.zip
and unzip it.
There is now a folder Forth2 including a few files.
Open this directory and start the **Forth2.exe** program.

As this program starts, it loads the file "forthvoc.vok" with the already defined vocabulary of Forth commands.

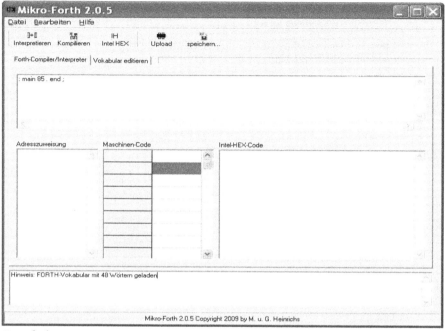

Translation:

File   Work on   Help
Interpret   Compile Intel HEX   Upload   Save
Forth Compiler/Interpreter   Edit Vocabulary
Address Allocation   Machine Code   Intel HEX Code

Picture 4: The main MikroForth Window

Our first program consists of just one short line of code:

```
: main  85  .  end ;
```

Enter this Forth source at the top of the form (**Picture 4**) under Forth Compiler/Interpreter. Do not forget the separating spaces between each command, especially after the colon and before the semicolon.

This input does not need to be completed with the RETURN key.

Our program first displays the number 85 at port B; Since the number 85 is written as 01010101 in the binary system, this should produce the desired pattern for the LEDs (see **Picture 3**).

The program then gets into an endless loop.
Next, we press the "Interpret" button.
We receive the following warning:

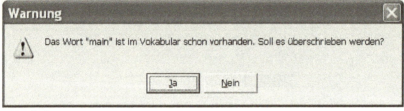

Translation:
Warning
The word "main" already exists in the vocabulary.Should it be overwritten?
Yes No

Picture 5: A warning. Decide if to overwrite or not

What does that mean?
"." or "**end**" are so-called words; They represent commands or command sequences to be executed by the microcontroller. The totality of all available words is called the Forth vocabulary.
When interpreting the line typed in, a new word "main" is added to the vocabulary, which contains the number **85** and the words "." and "**end**". Obviously, there was already a word "main" in the vocabulary.

As we shall see, creating new commands is an essential concept of the FORTH programming language.
Since the old word "main" – whatever its meaning was - is to be replaced with our new one, we click on "Yes" in the warning in **Picture 5**.
This new word "**main**" now needs the correct machine code for this microcontroller. To do this, we press the "Compile" button.
Our FORTH compiler obtains the program sections for the individual components of "main" from the file "forthvoc.vok" which are here the words "." and "**end**", and combines them into a new program.

In the address allocation area (**Picture 6**), see further down, the assignment of these subroutines to the specific program memory addresses can be seen; the line " . o $ 001A "means, for example:

The subroutine for".", which is responsible for the output on port B, and it starts at address 26 = $ 1A. The entire program is then displayed in the machine code area. Under each address, we find a machine code word consisting of 2 bytes.
In this logbook area we find further entries; the meaning of those will be discussed later on.

As shown in the machine code area, the program is stored in the microcontroller (if one does not take into account that the higher-order byte of a machine code word is not stored before in the memory of the microcontroller, but rather behind in the low-order one).

However, most programmers use a different format, which includes additional control bytes: the Intel HEX format. With the "Intel-HEX" button, we are now converting our machine code into this format. The Intel HEX code appears immediately in the Intel HEX area (**Picture 6**).

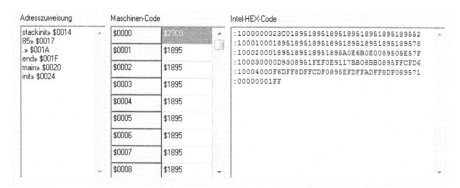

Translation:

Address Allocation	Machine Code	Intel Hex Code

Picture 6: Adress allocation of the machine code and the resulting Intel HEX code for programming the microcontroller

Finally, we need to load this code into the Attiny. The Uploader program is used again with our ATtiny board. We call it by pressing the "Upload" button; The Intel HEX code is then automatically handed over to the Uploader program and can be transferred to the ATtiny in the usual way.

If you have not made any input error when typing, the LEDs have been inserted correctly into the sockets, the battery is still full and the transmission has worked smoothly, yes – then the bit pattern from Picture 1 should be displayed and we congratulate you on the successful implementation.

Your first FORTH program sucessfully finished and running!

3 Defining Words

In order for a microcontroller to fulfil a specific task, one must provide the appropriate commands. So far in the past, we had used the programming language BASCOM or the assembler of the Atmel AVR series. Now we want to show you how to use our MicroForth system.

FORTH commands are called words. Such words can be grouped into types of commands; and new words arise. The totality of all words available to FORTH is called the vocabulary. When you create a new word, it basically means an extension of the existing vocabulary.
Using the example of a traffic light program, we want to illustrate this. For the sake of simplification, we leave out the red-yellow phase of the normal German traffic light.

```
: ampelzyklus   rotphase grünphase gelbphase ;
: Tr_LightCyc redphase greephase yellowphase ;
```

Our FORTH compiler basically works in two steps. During the first step, the entered source code is interpreted. The part of the FORTH program, which is responsible here, is called the interpreter.
In our case, the interpreter first encounters the double point; this shows that a new word with the name ampelzyklus is to be generated. This word consists of the following commands: redphase, greenphase, and yellowphase. The semicolon at the end indicates to the interpreter the end of the command sequence.
As our interpreter basically allows only one word definition per line, we could actually do without the semicolon. But other FORTH compilers also allow multiple word definitions per line, and then the semicolon as a limiter becomes indispensable. So we stay compatible.

A new word is generally defined as follows:
Colon definition

```
: <Name of new word>   <command sequence with already defined words> ;
```

All words, including the colon and the semicolon, must be separated by at least one space.

Let's test our first word-creation: We start the program Forth2 and enter the FORTH-source code. Capital or not - MikroForth does not care.

Then press the Interpret button. The following messages appear immediately in the status field at the bottom of the Forth2 window:

```
Fehler: Das Wort "rotphase" wurde im Vokabular nicht gefunden. "ampelzyklus" wurde nicht im Vokabular eingetragen!
Warnung: Interpretiervorgang abgebrochen.
Hinweis: Ggf. existiert noch altes Wort "ampelzyklus" im Vokabular.
```

Error: The word "redphase" could not be found in the vocabulary. "ampelphase" has not been entered into the vocabulary.
Warning: Interpreting Cycle has been stopped.
Hint: possibly there still exists an old word " ampelzyklus" in the vocabulary.

Picture 7: Errors and warnings

What do they mean? The first message is an error message. Errors usually lead to the termination of an operation. In this case, the next warning indicates that the interpreting process has been interrupted.
In order to eliminate our mistake, we must find its cause. Obviously, our FORTH system does not know the word rotphase. This is not too bad, because we can eliminate this "error" by making up a new definition of redphase. To do so, we add the following line before defining ampelcycle:

```
: rotphase rotesLicht an warte rotesLicht aus ;
: Redphase red light on wait red light;
```

Now our FORTH system is no longer complaining about the word redphase, which is not found, but it reports that it can not find the word redlight. So we have to define this word. The same applies to the words greenphase, yellowphase, on, wait, off, as well as the words yellowlight and greenlight.

All of these definitions are already fixed and ready in the file ampel.frth.
Open this file with "File - Open". The source text looks as follows:

```
: InitializePortB 7 DDRB ;
: Wait 3 wait ;
```

```
: Redlight 2; : Yellowlight 1 ;
: Greenlight 0 ;
: On 1 outPortB ;
: From 0 outPortB ;
: Redphase     redlight      on wait
               Red light     off  ;
: Greenphase   greenlight    on wait
               Green light   off  ;
: Yellowphase  yellowlight   on wait
               Yellowlight   off  ;
: Ampelcycle   redphase greenphase yellowphase  ;
: Main initializePortB ampel ample cycle  ;
```

To ensure, that the interpreter no longer reports any errors, our new words have to be – via intermediate steps – be traced back to words that are already have in the vocabulary. In this case, these are the numbers **0, 1, 2, 3** and **7** (these can also be viewed as words), as well as the words **wait**, **DDRB**, and **outPortB**.

The word **wait** causes the ATtiny to wait, **outPortB** outputs values on port B, and **DDRB** sets the data direction register of PortB. How these three words work in detail, will be looked at in the next chapters. At the moment only one thing should be clear:
Complex words like our word **ampelcycle** can be traced step by step down to elementary words. This approach is also called **top-down programming**.
We could, of course, have been able to do exactly the opposite: starting off with the elementary words, we could have defined increasingly complex words, until we had finally come to status of our word ampelcycle. This approach is called **bottom-up programming**.

In practice, one often works with both methods at the same time.

However, one point is very important for us:
Words that are used to define a new word must have already been defined before. This means, that they must already belong to the FORTH basic vocabulary or have been defined in the preceding code lines; and they must have already been added to the vocabulary when starting to interpret. The added basic words must therefore always be at the top in the FORTH source code, the derived ones below.
Regardless, of whether we use the top-down method or the bottom-up method, the problem to be solved by programming a traffic light system has to be gradually broken down into many small sub-problems.

Such subproblems are also called modules and the decomposition itself is called modularization or factoring. Modularization is an essential feature of the FORTH programming language. Good FORTH programs are characterized by the fact that the individual word definitions form meaningful units and are not too long. Of course, the selected word names should also be meaningful.

Let's look at the source text again. Does it meet the criteria of a good FORTH code? Certainly the first lines, however short they may be, the meaning is not immediately obvious; But this is due to the fact that we do not know enough about the words **wait**, **DDRB** and **outPortB**.

Word sequences such as

```
greenlight on wait greenlight off
```

Can easily be understood even without any programming knowledge.
The most important word in the entire source text we have not yet discussed; It is the word **main**. When the ATtiny is switched on, it always starts with the execution of exactly this word. The word **main** thus has the meaning of a main program; Therefore also the choice of the word name "**main**". All actions that the microcontroller is supposed to execute must ultimately originate from this word.

Thus, the source text must always end with the definition of **main**, and when interpreting, one must always allow the overwriting an already existing **main** word; Otherwise FORTH would work with such an old "main program" that had been defined before. And this may not have anything to do with our traffic light control.
In our case we see as the last line of our program:

```
: main initPortB AmpleCycle AmpleCycle ;
```

This means: The ATtiny first initializes Port B and then executes two full traffic light cycles.
In the meantime, you have probably no longer been able to resist the temptation and have the source text of our complete traffic light program been interpreted. If you have not changed anything, the status field should now show that the existing word **main** (already in the vocabulary) has been overwritten as desired.
This part of the programming, which is the most complicated for us has been done now|: The source text has been created and the newly defined words have been added into the vocabulary. Now our FORTH system has to start its work: These words must be translated into ATtiny machine code. This step is called **compiling**. How this

compilation works in detail, can be quite well understood with FORTH. In a later chapter, we shall discuss this in more detail.

For now, let's take the easy route: we press the **compile button** and as next step then the **Intel HEX code button**. The HEX code is finally transferred to the Attiny as usual by using the uploader program.

We had there already installed the necessary hardware on our board: a red LED at PortB.2, one yellow one at PortB.1 and a green LED at PortB.0.
Try it out yourself. We are sure you can also observe the two traffic light cycles on your Attiny board.

Task 1:
Take the existing file ampel.frth and modify/create a "German type traffic light" with the additional red-yellow phase.

4 Working with the Stack

The stack is one of the most important concepts of FORTH. We can imagine a stack of numbers as a pile of plates. What is the purpose of such a stack and how is it used? This will be explained in this chapter.
Let us first look at the Forth word stack:

```
: Stack   11   22   33   44   55   ;
```

If this word is executed, then the numbers **11, 22, 33, 44** and **55** are placed on the stack one by one. We can imagine this:

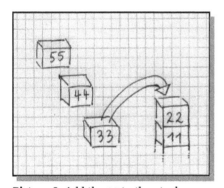

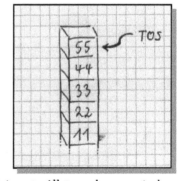

Picture 8: Add the 33 to the stack   **Picture 9:** All 5 numbers on stack

In the end, our five numbers lie on top of each other, the 11 on the lowest location, the 55 on top. The top number is also called TOS (Top Of Stack).
Words such as, for example, "." and **wait** will access this stack. The word "." takes the TOS from the stack and outputs that number on port B; the word **wait** also grabs a number from TOS, the waiting time, and delays further activity for the corresponding number of seconds.
If the following word

```
: output   .   wait   .   ;
```

is executed after the word **stack**, the following happens:
"." Retrieves the number **55** from the stack and outputs it to port B.

wait retrieves the number **44** from the stack and waits for a corresponding number of seconds.

"**.**" retrieves the number **33** from the stack and outputs it to port B.

At the end, only the numbers **11** and **22** stay on the stack.

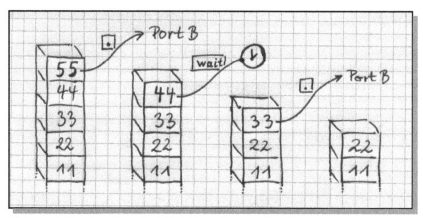

Picture 10: Number 55 to Port B, 44 to wait, 33 to Port B

Words change the status of the Stack: our word **stack** puts 5 numbers on the stack, our word **output** removes the top three numbers.

Some words first retrieve numbers from the stack and then create new values for the stack. This is especially true for calculating operations such as plus and minus.

Let's take a closer look at how to use the word "+" in FORTH to add two numbers. For example, the numbers **4** and **9** are to be added. From most pocket calculators, but also from many programming languages, one is accustomed to write the following statement:

4 + 9

The + sign is placed between the two numbers; This notation is called Infix Notation. In FORTH you write this as follows:

4 9 +   (do not forget the spaces between 4 and 9

First, the two numbers are entered here and then the + sign is the last character: this is referred to as Postfix Notation.

What is hidden here? Of course our stack and how it works! First, the numbers 4 and 9 are placed onto the stack; Then, the word "+" fetches these two numbers from the stack, adds them, and puts the result (that is, 13) back on the stack.

The advantage here is that the word "+" in FORTH immediately executes the addition; Both values are already present.

Using Infix Notation is not so easy. Here, pocket calculators or computers must first store the + somewhere; the actual addition can only be carried out after the second number has been entered, and then as well another command, for example in the form of "=".
Let us use our knowledge to make the ATtiny with FORTH the computational task of **4 + 9**. Our program looks like this:

```
: Main   4   9   +   .   ;
```

We enter this word into the source text field, interpret, compile, and transfer it. The Light Emitting Diodes at Port B actually indicate the number 13 (& B00001101 = 8 + 4 + 1).

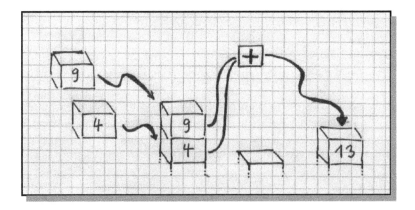

Picture 11: 4 onto stack – 9 onto stack – add them and put the result onto the stack

We have already learned in detail what happens here: First, the numbers **4** and **9** are placed on the stack; Then the word "+" fetches these two numbers from the stack, adds them, and returns the result to the stack. The next word "." gets this number **13** from the stack and outputs it to Port B.

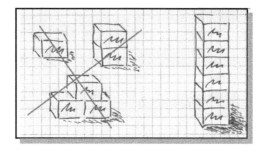

Picture 12: Not different market stalls – but all on one stack

We can see: The stack is a sort of marketplace, where the individual words can get or even give out numbers. In contrast to a real market place, however, only numbers can be traded here.

In addition, there is only one stand here, and at this stand, the numbers are not somehow placed somewhere, but rather in a nice order of one on top of the other on one stack.

At this point we can already give one secret away: FORTH provides further possibilities for the exchange of data between the words, e.g. so-called Variables.

The exchange via the stack is however the most important method. That's why we want to practice more how to deal with the stack.

We have already learned how to solve simple computing tasks in FORTH. But what about more complex ones?

Example 1:
```
Term:    (3 + 5) * 2
FORTH:    3 5 + 2 *
```

Example 2:
```
Term:    120-5 * 20
FORTH:   120  5  20  *  -
```

Looking at the last example, the numbers 120, 5, and 20 might already be on the stack; to get the result only the words "*" and "-" would have to be executed in succession. Is this also the case in the first example? No, it would not be as simple as in Example 2: As the number 2 is on the TOS, each operation would in any case refer to this number first. However, the brackets in this term require, that the numbers 3 and 5 are first processed (added).

There are, however, a number of pre-defined Forth words which will manipulate the numbers on the stack – exchange them, delete them, duplicate them.

5 Port Control Commands

MikroForth provides the following port commands:

Word	Type	Comment	Stack
.	A	Sends the TOS to Port B; (Data Direction bits of Port B are all set before to 1 / Output)	(n –)
blink	F	b hp blink sends the bit pattern of b to Port B, waits for hp milliseconds, sends 0 to Port B and waits again for hp milliseconds.	(b hp –)
DDBitB	A	bit flag DDBitB sets the *bit* of Ports B to Output, if *flag* = 1, else to Input.	(bit flag –)
DDBitD	A	**bit flag DDBitD** sets the *bit* of Ports D to Output, if *flag* = 1, else to Input.	(bit flag –)
DDRB	A	Writes b into the Data Direction Register of Port B.	(b –)
DDRD	A	Writes d into the Data Direction Register of Port D.	(d –)

InPortB	A	bit InPortB reads the Input bit of Port B, and puts 0/1 if the Input Bit is High or Low. See DDRB and DDBitB	(bit – flag)
InPortD	A	bit InPortD Reads the Input of bit at Port D and puts the value as 0 or 1 onto the stack. See DDRD and DDBitD	(bit – flag)
Word	**Type**	**Comment**	**Stack**
outPortB	A	bit flag outPortB Sets the relevant Output bit of Port B to High or Low if the flag on stack is 0 or 1. See DDRB and DDBitB	(bit flag –)
outPortD	A	bit flag outPortD Sets the relevant Output bit of Port D to High or Low if the flag on stack is 0 or 1. See DDRD and DDBitD	(bit flag –)
Ta0?	F	Puts 1/0 onto the stack, if switch Ta0? is open/closed (D2=1/0) PortD.2 is configured automatically.	(– bit)
Ta1?	F	Puts 1/0 onto the stack, if switch Ta1? is open/closed (D3=1/0) PortD.3 is configured automatically.	

As examples, we will use the words ".", **blink, Ta0?, DDBitD, OutPortD**, and **InPortD**. The remaining words are very similar in their meaning.

To use more interesting examples, however, we would like to introduce a simple FORTH loop construction: the **BEGIN UNTIL** loop. It looks as follows:

```
Begin    Bef1 Bef2 Bef3 ... until
```

The commands **Bef1**, **Bef2**, **Bef3**, ... are executed in repeated sequence. However, this happens only until the word **until** finds a 0 on the TOS.
To be more specific, the word **until** takes the value from the TOS and checks if it is 0 or 1.

If it is 0 (FALSE), then the loop is executed again;
If it is 1 (TRUE), then the loop is terminated.
If you write a 0 immediately before the word **until** is executed, then an infinite loop is formed:

```
: Endless  Bef1  Bef2  Bef3 ... 0  until ;
```

Let's have a look at our first example:
All LEDs on Port B should go on and off at intervals of 100 ms.
The program for this is quite simple:

```
: Main  begin  255  .  100  waitms  0  .
        100  waitms  0  until  ;
```

Let us look at the definition of **main** word by word.
Begin initiates the infinite loop bounded by 0 until.
Within the loop, **255** is first placed on the stack.
This number is immediately taken from the stack by the word "."
    and output to port B.
    Port B is automatically configured as an output by ".";
    Which means as well that DDRB has been set to & B11111111.

All LEDs on port B are now switched on via the 255.
After this, the number **100** is placed on the stack
to be immediately fetched by the word "**waitms**
    the microcontroller is now waiting for 100 ms.

Subsequently, the number **0** is output on the port B;
 The LEDs are all switched off.

Then the microcontroller waits for 100 ms.

We have now arrived at the end of our heavy work.

Now the whole sequence starts again from the beginning   and so on and so on ... Our LEDs at Port B are flashing continuously.

In our second example, an LED on PortD.6 should be switched off and on by using the button Ta0. Specifically, this LED should be off as long as the push-button Ta0 is pressed, and light up while the push-button is not pressed.

The necessary FORTH program can be formed by the following lines:

```
: switch   begin Ta0? 6 swap
           OutPortD 0 until  ;
: prepare 6 1 DDBitD  ;
: main     prepare switch  ;
```

First, via the word **prepare,** bit 6 of the data direction register of D is set to **1;** Port D.6 is thus configured as an output.

The word **switch** consists of an endless loop.

At the beginning of the loop, the word **Ta0?** checks whether the button **Ta0** is pressed or not. If Ta0 is pressed, it places the value **0** onto the stack, otherwise the value **1.**

Similar. As explained with the word ".", the corresponding input port bit D.2 is configured via the word **Ta0?** automatically (input and pull-up).

Next, the number **6** is placed onto the stack; **swap** exchanges this value **6** with the on-off value value supplied by **Ta0?.**

Now the bit value **6** and the on-off value are exactly in the order on the stack as required by **OutPortD**: the bit value at the bottom and the on-off value at the top (in the vocabulary named a flag).

6 1 OutPortD switches the LED on at PortD.6 on;
6 0 OutPortD turns it off.

Note: Only for the words ".", **Ta0?, Ta1?** and **blink** include an automatic configuration of the ports;

In all other cases, the data direction bytes or bits must be set by the user with the help of the words DDRB, DDRD, DDBitB and DDBitD.

In a third example, a loop of a flashing bit pattern is to be interrupted by the button Ta0. In this example, the bit pattern 01010101 is to be switched on and off until the button Ta0 is pressed. The corresponding program is again very short and looks like this:

```
: main  begin 85 100 blink Ta0? not until ;
```

Within the **BEGIN UNTIL** loop, the blink word using the bit pattern &B01010101 = 85 and the half period duration of 100 ms is first executed.

Subsequently, with **Ta0?** the state of the button Ta0 is interrogated; if this button is pressed, a **0** is placed on the stack, otherwise a **1**.

Without the following word **not** , this on - off value of the button would be evaluated directly by **until**: the status value 0 (pressed button) would lead to a further loop run and the status value 1 (pushbutton open) would abort the loop. The loop would thus be terminated by an opening and not - as required - by the closing the button.

In order to get to a correctly functioning program, the status value must be inverted: A value of **1** must be changed into a **0** and a value of **0** into a **1**.

This can be achieved via the word **not**: This word retrieves the state value from the stack and replaces it with its logical complement. The word sequence **Ta0? not** now returns the value **0** as required on the TOS when the button is open and the value 1 when the button is pressed.

Task 1:
A look into the FORTH editor shows how the word **Ta0?** Is defined:

```
: Ta0?  2  0  DDBitD  2  1  outPortD  2 InPortD  ;
```

Explain this definition.

Task 2:
How could the program of the first example be simplified using the word **blink** ?

Task 3:

Change the program of the second example so that the LED lights up when the button is pressed, and not lit otherwise.

Task 4:

The ATtiny is to show the number of push button activities of Ta0 at the button at PortB; for this, PortB must be equipped with 8 LEDs. Note: To push the button always takes a certain time. Even in the case of a quick push by a human, the button remains closed for several milliseconds, and for the ATtiny it is a half an eternity!

6 Loops and Branches

You have already learned about the first loop type in the chapter on the port commands, the **BEGIN-UNTIL** loop. It has the following form:

begin   Bef1 Bef2 Bef3 ... until

Using this construction, the instruction sequence between **begin** and **until** is executed until the word **until** finds a 1 on the TOS. **1** is generally interpreted as TRUE, **0** as FALSE. The loop is therefore executed until the truth value is TRUE on the stack. Note that until also gets the value from the TOS; It must therefore be ensured that a suitable truth value is placed on the stack for the word until.

Since some practical examples of the BEGIN-UNTIL loop have already been presented in the chapter on the port commands, let us turn to the next loop type, the counting loop. In FORTH it looks as follows:

ew sw do   Bef1 Bef2 Bef3 ... loop.

The identifiers **ew** (end value) and **sw** (start value) are here for the value of the loop index at the last or first grinding run. Within the counting loop, ie between the words do and loop, one can access the loop index using the word **I**: **I** places the current loop index on the stack. Let's look at a simple example:

: count 25 10 do I. 100 waitms loop;

For this word, the counting loop starts with the index 10. This number is first placed on the stack by the word I and the word. At port B. *** " After a wait of 100 milliseconds, the loop index is automatically increased and the loop continues to run through. The loop will loop through the last time the loop index is 25. So our program counts at a tenth of a second from 10 to 25 and then stops.

When specifying the values for the loop index, note the order: First the end value and then the start value are specified.

As a further example, consider the FORTH definition of multiplication:

: * 0 swap 1 do swap dup red + loop;

If the main program is, B.

: Main 12 7 *. ;

The number 12 is added a total of 7 times to 0; The multiplication is thus attributed to a multiple addition. As is the case in detail, the reader should consider himself by stating the content of the stack for each individual step.

Our MikroForth has only one branch type, the skipIf statement. This word first evaluates the TOS; If the value 1 (TRUE) is on the TOS, the next statement is skipped. If the value 0 (FALSE) is on the TOS, the next command (word) is simply processed.

1 skipIf Bef1 Bef2 Bef3 ...

Here, after the word skipIf, the word Bef1 is skipped and immediately further processed with the word Bef2.

This is followed by the word Bef3, etc.

0 skipIf Bef1 Bef2 Bef3 ...

Here, after the word skipIf, the word Bef1 is used. The following are the words "Bef2" and "Bef3".

Frequently, the truth values 0 and 1 are obtained as the results of comparisons. Comparators are used here. Similar to the arithmetic operators +, *, - and /, they are also used in postfix notation for FORTH. By

7 2 >

It is therefore checked whether 7 > 2. Since this is true in this case, the value 1 (TRUE) is placed on the stack as a result of this comparison operation. Further comparison operators are <and =.

An example is to explain how comparative operators and branches can be used sensibly. A measurement process may already have two measured values (eg temperature values) placed on the stack. As the name implies, the word difference is intended to determine the difference between the two numbers; For example, For example, be required to allow the microcontroller to initiate certain measures if this difference is too great.

Let us first consider the calculation and the output of the difference. At first glance, this problem seems to be quite easy to solve:

```
: difference - . ;
```

For test purposes we use our Forth compiler:

```
: Main 7 2 differed ;
```

After interpreting, compiling and transmitting, our microcontroller displays the value 5 - as expected! Now we enter the measured values once in reverse order:

```
: Main 2 7 difference ;
```

The microcontroller amPort B now displays the value 251 (!). How can this obviously nonsensical result be explained and, at least as importantly, how can our program be improved?

First, the explanation: With the subtraction 2 - 7, the microcontroller reaches the range below 0. It works as a kilometer counter: If one goes out from the kilometer distance 0002 now 7 km backwards, one reaches the position of 9995. The mileage is jumping from 0000 to 9999. The microcontroller works quite similarly: it jumps from 000 to 255 when counting downwards.

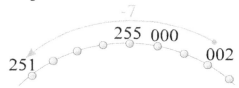

Picture 13: Subtraction results

The problem is obviously in the order of the two measured values. In order to improve the program, we must ensure that the measured values are exchanged when the first measured value is smaller than the second. Here, our skipIf word can be used; For the corresponding comparison, the measured values have to be copied beforehand
: difference over over > skipIf swap - . ;
The following stack picture shows what is happening in different ways.

$$a\ b \rightarrow a\ b\ a \rightarrow a\ b\ a\ b \rightarrow a\ b\ \text{flag}$$
flag = 1 → a - b
flag = 0 → b a → b - a
→ *Ausgabe*

Task 1:
If the difference between the two measured values on the stack is greater than 3, a warning tone should be output via D.6 and the beeper.

Task 2:
Write a definition for the FORTH word "<=." Task 3How is the FORTH definition for the word not?

7 Keeping everything under Control: COM, I2C and EEPROM

Microcontrollers are often used as the heart of autonomous measuring stations. They should meet the following requirements:

1.   You must have a memory which can safely store the measured data – even if the electrical supply to the microcontroller fails.

2.   You must have a common communication interface to sensors.

3.   They must have communication interfaces to terminals, so that the data can be easily transferred to computers for further evaluation.

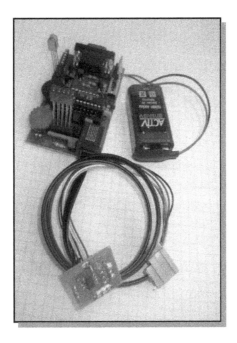

Figure 14: A complete application system: The Board with MikroForth, USB-to-TTL-converter and battery

All of this can be done using our ATtiny2313 and MikroForth: there is an EEPROM, which can store data permanently without an active power supply. Via the I2C bus it can communicate with sensors and other devices and via the COM interface the Attiny2313 can send the stored data to another computing device via a serial interface. For more detailed explanations regarding the EEPROM, I2C and COM interface, please refer to the relevant sections in this document or the data sheet at

http://www.atmel.com/Images/Atmel-2543-AVR-ATtiny2313_Summary.pdf for the 20 page summary

http://www.atmel.com/images/doc8246.pdf for all details, 200+ pages.

Here, we now use a simple example to illustrate how MicroForth can be used to make a sequence of temperature measurements.

The structure is simple: A temperature sensor LM75 with the I2C address 157 is connected to the I2C socket of the Attiny board (**Picture 14**). Remember to set the jumpers required to pull up the two lines SDA and SCL. The data is exchanged with the PC via the same cable as used for the programming.

The following FORTH words are provided by MikroForth for communicating with EEPROM, I2C and COM:

Word	Type	Comment	Stack
>com	A	Sends TOS to the COM Interface. Before, the COM Interface has to be initialized by using the word INITCOM	(n –)
>eprom	A	Writes the value w to address a of the EEPROM. See eprom>	(w a –)
Wort	Typ	Kommentar	Stack
com>	A	Takes the byte received via the serial COM interface and puts it onto the stack. See >com.	(– n)

eprom>	A	Reads the value w from the EEPROM address a, and copies the value onto the stack. See >eprom	(a – w)
i2cread	A	A value is read from the I2C slave; when ACK = 0, an Acknowledge Signal is sent.	(ACK – Wert)
i2cstart	A	The Start signal for the I²C-Bus is sent. (SDA changes from 1 to 0; then SCL from 1 to 0)	(–)
i2cstop	A	Initializes the I²C Bus (SCL and SDA to 1); The Data Direction bits for SDA (PortB.5) und SCL (PortB.7) are set.	(–)
i2cwrite	A	One single Byte (value or address) are sent to the slave; The Acknowledge Bit is put onto the stack.	(Wert/Adr – ACK)
initCom	A	Initializes the COM Interface: D0 = RxD D1 = TxD Baud rate = 9600 8 Bit No parity	(–)

First, we look at the measurement process: The ATtiny has to record 20 temperature values in the EEPROM at 1 second intervals for 20 seconds. This is achieved using the two words **measure** and **main**:

```
: measure   i2cstop  i2cstart  1   wait
            157  i2cwrite  1  i2cread ;
: main 20 1 do measurement I> eprom loop ;
```

Let's start by looking at the definition of **measure**:

i2cstop initializes the I2C interface (SCL and SDA to high),

i2cstart gives the start signal (SDA changes from high to low);

157 i2cwrite is used to address our temperature sensor.

Finally, with **1 I2cread**, a temperature value from the LM75 is asked for and placed on the stack;

The parameter **1** ensures, that no acknowledge signal is given. An Acknowledge would cause the LM75 to send next the decimal point. Note also, that the LM75 requires up to 300 ms for a single temperature measurement. A longer pause (here 1 second) between the individual measurements is therefore really necessary!

The **main** word consists essentially of a counting loop, and the individual measured values are stored into the EEPROM. The loop index **I** indicates the address value in the EEPROM.

Now we have to transfer the measured values from the EEPROM of the 2313 to the PC. To do this, we use the word **eprom2com**:

```
: Eprom2com eprom>> com 1 waitms ;
```

```
: main initCom 20 1 do I eprom2com loop;
```

Before this data can be transferred, byte by byte, via the COM interface, it must first be initialized. This is done with the word **initCom**.

When sending the bytes, the timing of the transfer protocol must be considered: The transfer of a byte via the serial interface takes a certain amount of time. During this transmission process, however, the microcontroller is already processing its program.

If you omit the command **1 waitms**, the microcontroller would want to start the next transmission before the last byte has been completely transmitted.

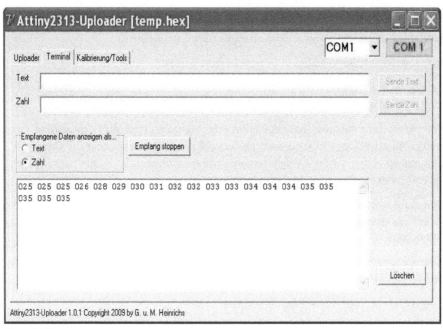

Translation:

                                                  COM selection

Uploader   Terminal   Calibration/Tools
Text
Number
Display received data   Stop receiving of data
Text
Number

Picture 15: The Uploader software

If we now run the UPLOADER terminal program, all measured values are transmitted to the computer in less than one second. **Picture 15** shows the result of such a transmission. It can clearly be seen, that the temperature values initially remain constant and then rapidly increase. How could this happen?

During this measurement, a lamp was held directly over the LM75; This was greatly enhanced mt. In **Picture 16** you can see the results as a graph converted by using a standard spreadsheet program.

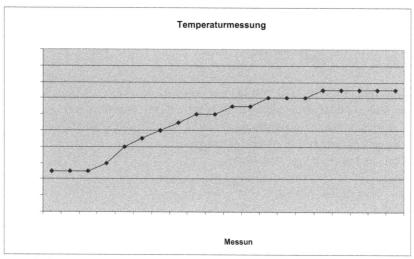

Translation: Temperature measurement

Picture 16: Logging data

8 MikroForth Variables

The stack is ideally suited for short-term storage and transfer of values from one word to another. The EEPROM of the ATtiny is more suitable for long-term storage.
However, it is quite tedious to remember the different addresses where the values are stored. The remedy here is the creation of variables.
They are declared as follows in MikroForth:

`Variable <variable name>`

The variable can not be declared within a double-point definition; The key word **variable** must be at the beginning of a line. You can only declare one single variable at a time, and there is no semicolon at the end of the declaration.

The compiler will assign a number between 0 and 126 for each variable, which serves as the EEPROM address; the EEPROM cell with address 127 is reserved for the OSCCAL value. In addition, the compiler generates a word with the given name for each variable. This word has only one task: it places the corresponding address onto the stack.

For example, let's look at the use of variables:

```
Variable accountno
: store 129 accountno >eprom ;
: get accountno eprom> ;
: main store get . ;
```

The first line declares the variable **accountno**.
In the second line, the corresponding address is placed onto the stack. If **accountno** had been declared as the first variable, then this address would have been $ 00.

The following word **>eprom** takes the number 129 from the stack and stores it at EEPROM address $00.

In our third line, the number 129 is retrieved from the EEPROM at cell $00 and is placed onto the stack.

The word **accountno** can be viewed here as a substitute of the associated EEPROM address.

The introduction of variables does not substantially change the source code; But it becomes a lot less complex.
Note: Since only a limited number of write cycles are allowed for an EEPROM cell, we should use these variable words rather sparingly.

Therefore, the MikroForth variables should be considered more as constants – written once but can be read as often as needed.

In principle, the variables could also be used to address SRAM or Flash memory. This is however not recommended here at all. The compiler assigns addresses in sequence, beginning with $00. For this reason it is almost certain that uncontrolled important status registers or even parts of the program would be overwritten in this way. The consequences would be fatal.

Task 1:
Enter the above example and test it. Look at the word **acountno** using the Vocabulary Editor.

9 The MikroForth Compiler

FORTH has a rather simple structure as a language; therefore, it is not so difficult to understand the functioning of our Forth compiler. The starting point of our considerations is a small FORTH program, which we already know from the chapter on the port commands, the file is called "schalten.frth":

```
: turnon begin Ta0? 6 swap outPortD 0 until ;
: prepare 6 1 DDBitD ;
: main prepare switch ;
```

This program turns on and off a light emitting diode connected to port D.6 and using the push-button Ta0.
We open this file and press the Interpret button. In this way, the new words of the double point definitions are entered into the vocabulary. We can easily check this by clicking on the "Edit Vocabulary" tab in the upper left corner.

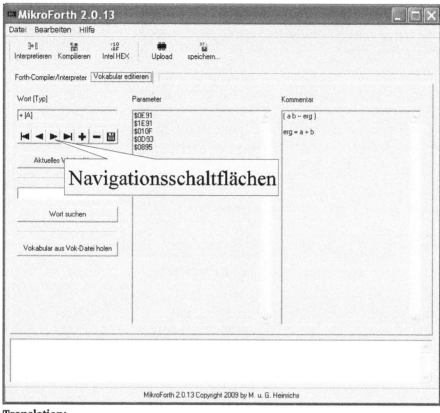

Translation:

File   Work on   Help
Interpret   Compile   Intel HEX   Upload   Save
Forth Compiler/Interpreter   Edit Vocabulary
Word (Type)   Parameter   Comment
Navigation Buttons
Current Word
Search Word
Get Vocabulary from VOK-File

Picture 17: The MikroForth screen

In this editor, we can look at all of the words in the vocabulary; In addition, we can also modify existing words or even create new words, but we will discuss this in a later chapter.

If we now press the button ⏭, we reach the last word of the vocabulary; here we find our word "**prepare**". In the parameter field, we discover the words by which **prepare** has been described within the scope of the double-point definition.

When interpreting, the text is essentially only restructured: from a text line, the defined word and the associated parameters are peeled out.

We can also look at the new word **switchon**, we only need to press the button ◀; via this, we reach the one before last word of the vocabulary.

By pressing this button again and again, we can look at all of the words in the vocabulary.
It can be seen that there are two types of words:

1. **F-Words:**
   Their parameters are composed again from words.
   They have emerged from double point definitions.

2. **A-Words:**
   Their parameters consist of machine code.
   This machine code was generated using an assembler.

As our microcontroller can process machine code only, the entire FORTH source code must be brought back to such A-words. This is the task of the compiler. To see how this is executed, we will now take a closer look at the example above.

To do this, click on the tab "**Compiler / Interpreter**" and return to the familiar MikroForth mode.

The starting point for our considerations is first the word **main**. With this word the microcontroller will start its work. The word **main** calls the words **prepare** and **switchon**.

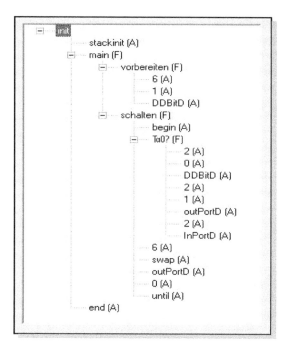

Picture 18: Where to find the different A and F Words

The parameters of **prepare** are all A–words; on the other hand, the F–word **Ta0?** is included. This must again be analyzed; it only consists of A–words.

Such analysis can be illustrated in the form of a tree. **Picture 18** shows the tree for our program. However, the root of our tree does not consist of the word **main** as expected, but of the word **init**. This has the following reason: regardless of the special tasks that a FORTH program has to execute, there are certain tasks which are always to be done first.

In our case, before the execution of **main**, the stack must be set up; this is done by the word **stackinit**. After the execution of **main**, the microcontroller should always go into an infinite loop; the word **end**. Of course, this task could have been left to the user, but it is more comfortable and safer as implemented here.

The word **init** calls first **stackinit**, then the word **main** and finally the word **end**. If necessary, even the word **init** could be supplemented by additional standard tasks by overwriting the existing word **init** with a new one.

If you now press the "**Compile**" button, the tree from **Picture 18** is searched recursively for A-words; The associated parameters, i.e. the corresponding machine codes, are entered into the machine code table. The start address of these machine programs is additionally recorded in the **address allocation table**. Using this assignment table, a check is possible whether an A word has already been entered (compiled) or not; In this way it is avoided, that the same word is compiled several times.

The machine programs of all A-words end with the **ret** command (code $0895). Therefore, they can be called as subroutines. When compiling these F-words, the A-words that will appear as parameters, are replaced by corresponding subroutine calls. The parameters

```
6
1
DDBitD
```

of the word "**prepare**" generate the code

```
rcall
<Address of 6>
rcall
<address of 1>
rcall
<address of DDBitD>
ret
```

in an already assembled form.

Again, the address assignment table is used. As we can see, this program section also ends with a **ret** command; So, this part of the program can also be called up as a subroutine. The compiler executes exactly this process when, in a second run, it searches the tree for F-words. They are then entered in the address assignment table and the machine code table depending on the order and the search depth.

For example, the word **Tao?** Is entered before the word **switchon**; it is actually located behind the word **switchon**, but it is located deeper in the search tree.
To get from this machine code table to the HEX code, it is only a small step. In a sense, it means only a different way of spelling it. In fact, to burn the controller, this step must even be reversed.

It is very instructive to look at the results of such a compilation process in detail. For this, however, we do not look at the machine code itself but rather the associated assembler code; This can be generated from the HEX code using a so-called disassembler.

However here, we use a somewhat shorter example:

FORTH source code:
: **Main**   5   5   +   .   ;

HEX code:
```
: 1000000029C018951895189518951895189518954C
: 100010001895189518951895189518951895189578
: 100020001895189518951895A0E6B0E0089505E084
: 100030000D9308950E911E91010F0D9308951FEFDA
: 100040000E9117BB08BB0895FFCFF1DFF0DFF2DFA1
: 0C005000F6DF0895E9DFF9DFF7DF08951F
: 00000001FF
```

Assembler code:

```
                    rjmp    avr002A
                    reti
                    reti
                    reti
                    reti
                    reti
                    reti
                    reti
                    reti
                    reti
                    reti
                    reti
                    reti
                    reti
                    reti
                    reti
                    reti
                    reti
                    reti
                    reti
    avr0014:        ldi     XL, 0x60
                    ldi     XH, 0x00
                    ret
    avr0017:        ldi     r16, 0x05
                    st      X+, r16
                    ret
    avr001A:        ld      r16, -X
                    ld      r17, -X
                    add     r16, r17
                    st      X+, r16
                    ret
    avr001F:        ldi     r17, 0xFF
                    ld      r16, -X
                    out     DDRB, r17
                    out     PORTB, r16
                    ret
    avr0024:        rjmp    $
    avr0025:        rcall   avr0017
                    rcall   avr0017
                    rcall   avr001A
                    rcall   avr001F
                    ret
    avr002A:        rcall   avr0014
                    rcall   avr0025
                    rcall   avr0024
                    ret
```

Picture 19: AVR Assembler code snippets

The program starts with the command **rjmp $002A,** a jump to address $002A. (The following **reti** instruction we skip for now, and we shall discuss the meaning of the interrupts in detail later.)

At address $002A starts the subroutine of **init**:

```
Rcall $0014      ; stack init
Rcall $0025      ; main
Rcall $0024      ; end
```

Next, the **stackinit** subroutine is called; here, and the pointer for the stack is initialized; the register pair (XH, XL) is used as the pointer here. The stack pointer X is set to the value $0060; This is the lowest address of the SRAM.

Via the **ret** command the program jumps back to the next command of the **init** subroutine; here the **main** subroutine is called which starts at the address $0025. Since it is derived from a FORTH word, it itself consists of many subprogram calls, completed by a **ret** command.

The subroutine **it** at address $0017 is called twice. Here, the number **5** is placed on the stack. Here, this number **5** is initially buffered in register r16. Via the instruction sequence **st X+, r16** the contents of r16, that is, our number 5, is stored at the memory cell indexed by X by the command st X +, r16;

Then X is increased by 1, and is then pointing to the next memory location of the stack. Via the next two subroutine calls of **main**, the addition is executed (at address $001A) and the result is output to Port B (at $001F).

You can also see, how numbers are fetched from the stack: the command **ld r16, X-** for example: the value from the SRAM register indexed by X is fetched and put into the register r16 and the pointer value is decreased by 1; so X now points to the underlying stack content.

Last but not least, the subroutine **main** returns to the subroutine **init**. From here you continue with **rcall $0024**; And from there, the microcontroller is sent into an endless loop.

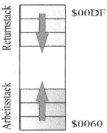

Picture 20: Parameter Stack growing upwards, Return Stack downwards

Anyone, who has dealt more closely with assembler subroutines, knows that another stack is used here, the so-called Return Stack. The stack, which we have looked at so far for FORTH programming, is often referred to as a parameter stack for distinction. Return Stack and Parameter Stack are both resident in SRAM.

They share it:
While the Parameter Stack starts at $0060 and then grows upwards, the Return Stack starts at $00DF and then grows in the direction of lower addresses (**Picture 20**). Organized in this way, the risk of a collision of the two stacks is kept as small as possible.

In contrast to the work stack, you do not have to worry about the management of the stackpointer Z of the return stack; This is taken care of by the instructions **rcall** and **ret** independently.

The essential idea of our Forth compiler is the interleaving of these subprograms. F-words consist only of subroutine calls; these can refer to F- or as well to A-words. Ultimately, these subroutine calls must of course always end up with A-words; only here the machine code can be found, which does not refer to another word, but actually does "work".

This simple concept naturally leads to limitations. Some control structures like IF ELSE-THEN or BEGIN-WHILE-REPEAT cannot be realized. On the other hand, this concept offers the possibility to insert new A-words into the vocabulary quite easily.
If you are interested in such options, you should jump to the one after next chapter.
In the next chapter, let us examine in more detail how control structures can be realized at all.

10 How the Do-Loop loop works

We will start from the following example:

    10 3 do Bef1 Find2 loop Bef3

This corresponds to the subroutine calls in memory:

    rcall <10>
    rcall <3>
    rcall <do>
    rcall <Bef1>
    rcall <Bef2>
    rcall <loop>
    rcall <Bef3>.

The pointed brackets mean "address of ...".

The start value (3) and the end value (10) of the loop index are placed on the work stack via the first two subroutines. Each time, the subroutine is called, the microcontroller saves the address of the next instruction by placing it on the return stack.

Thus, if the **do** subroutine is called, the address of **rcall <Bef1>** is placed onto the Return Stack. More specifically: this address consists of two bytes; We refer to these addresses as **AdrBef1** (high) and **AdrBef1** (low). Immediately after calling the **do** subroutine, our two stacks look like as shown in Picture 1 (20).

3
10

AdrBef1(high)
AdrBef1(low)

Arbeitsstack
Parameter Stack

Returnstack
Return Stack

Picture 21: Contents of Data Stack and Return Stack

All that the **do** subroutine has to do, is to ensure that the microcontroller stores this address pair for later; only in this way it can be ensured that it can return to the beginning of the loop from the end of a of the loop. The storing of this address can not be done via work registers, for example r16; The risk is, that this data could be overwritten for example, by the subroutine of **Bef1** or **Bef2**.

A safe place for remembering long-term is the Return Stack. Here, our address pair is already present, but at the end of the **do** subroutine, this address pair is pushed into the program counter by the **ret** command from the return stack and so disappears from the return stack.

However, the solution is also in sight: the address pair on the return stack must just be doubled by **do**; as result, the copy is still available after the execution of **do**. Additionally, the two loop indices must also be saved. This is accomplished by the following assembler code:

```
.def AdrH = r16
.def AdrL = r17
.def A = r18
.def E = r19
ld A, -x        ;Start index from
                ; the parameter stack
Ld E, -x        ;Loop end from
                ; the parameter stack
Pop AdrH pop AdrL      ;Return address
                       ; from the return stack
Push AdrL push AdrH   ;And again onto it
                       ; (for LOOP)
Push E push A      ;Loop parameters on
                   ; return stacks
Push AdrL push AdrH    ;Return address again
                       ; onto the stack
ret             ;To the next command
```

Immediately before the **ret** command of the **do** subroutine and immediately afterwards the return stack looks like this:

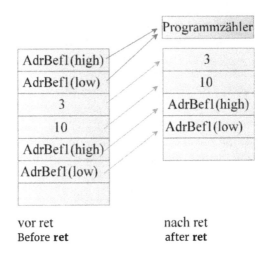

AdrBefl(high)			Programmzähler
AdrBefl(low)			3
3			10
10			AdrBefl(high)
AdrBefl(high)			AdrBefl(low)
AdrBefl(low)			

vor ret   nach ret
Before **ret**   after **ret**

Picture 22: Return Stack before and after Interrupt

The following subroutine call **rcall <Bef1>** now places the address pair of **rcall <Bef2>** on to the return stack; but it disappears when a return happens. And so it continues, until the following **loop** subroutine is called.

```
.def AdrH = r16        ; Return stack
.def AdrL = r17        ;
.def A = r18           ; Loop: current index
.def E = r19           ; End value of the loop index
.def nextAdrH = r20    ; Address of Bef3
.def nextAdrL = r21
pop nextAdrH pop nextAdrL    ; Save the address
                             ;  of Bef3
pop A                  ; Retrieve the current index
                             ;  from the return stack
pop E                  ; End value from the
                             ;  return stack
pop ZH                 ; Address of Bef1 from the return stack
pop ZL
cp A, E
breq loopende          ; If A = E then jump to loop end
                             ;  Otherwise (A < E)
push ZL                ; And again (for next LOOP)
push ZH
```

```
inc A          ;
push E
push A              ; Loop parameters on return stacks
ijmp                ; Jump to address, which is in Z
                    ; (see above); No additional add on stack!
loopende:
push nextAdrL
push nextAdrH;
ret                 ; To the next command
```

In this situation, the address pair of **rcall <Bef3>** is on the return stack. This pair is fetched first from the return stack and stored in work registers (**nextAdrH** and **nextAdrL**); The loop indices **3** and **10** are also stored in working registers (A and E, respectively).

The values **AdrBef1** (high) and **AdrBef1** (low) are shifted into the register pair Z; This will allow an indirect jump to the command **rcall <Bef1>**.
It is now checked whether the current loop index (**3**) is less than the final value (**10**). Since this is the case, the loop index (**3**) is increased by 1 to 4, the address pair and the indices for a possible further loop run are put back onto the return stack, and the indirect jump **ijmp** is executed. This leads to a jump to the address which is stored in the register pair Z, to **rcall <Bef1>**.

This is repeated until the current index value is equal to the final value (**10**). In this case, the buffered address pair of **rcall <Bef3>** is put back onto the return stack;
The program now jumps to the subroutine call of **Bef3** via the last command of **loop**, namely the **ret** command, as desired.
Task:
The word **do** can also be written as an F-word:

```
: Do   swap R> R> over >R
       >R rot >R rot >R R> R   ;
```

Look up the meaning of **R>** and **>R** in the vocabulary and see how this sequence of commands work by using the stack diagrams.

11 Creating A-Words

So far, we have only been concerned about how to create F-words. This was done by using the quote in the context of the usual interpretation and compilation process. For many applications, this is sufficient.

However, the words provided in the vocabulary may not be sufficient for certain applications. In this case, it is convenient to understand the problem accurately and to create a suitable A-word for it. Let us illustrate this in a simple example.

The task here should be, to create a word which outputs all of the values on the stack via the serial interface; such a word could well be used for test purposes. Loop structures and words for COM output and working with the SRAM are already available in our vocabulary. What is still missing is a word that indicates the number of values on the stack; This number is sometimes referred to as stack depth.

A new word **stackcount** has to be generated to determine this stack depth. For this purpose, the stack pointer X must be used; as this is not recorded by any of the existing Forth words, **stackcount** must be generated in machine code. We must therefore create an A-word.
The necessary assembler code looks like this:

```
.def stackcount = r16   ; R0 to r15 reserved for
                        ;  interrupts

mov stackcount, XL      ; Stackpointer XL to
                        ;  stackcount

Subi stackcount, $60 ; Subtract immediately
                        ; Stack start address $60

St x+, stackcount     ; Place result onto stack

ret                     ; and return
```

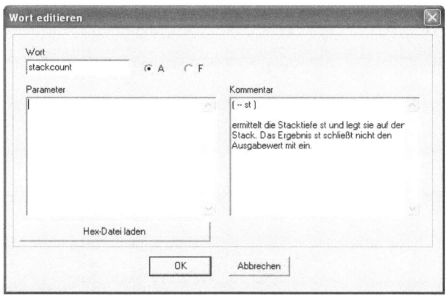

Translation:

Word   A-word or F-word

Parameter   Comment

Load HEX file

                              OK   Discard

Picture 23: Editing a and F Words

We run this code through the assembler, for example by using Studio 4, and save the hex file as "**stackcount.hex**". Now we open our program MikroForth and click on the button "edit vocabulary". Click the + button on the navigation bar; this opens a window for the editing of words; there we enter the name of the new word and as well the comment as shown in **Picture 23**.

Now we load this prepared hex code into the parameter field: To do this, we click the button "Load Hex file" below the parameter field and open our file "**stackcount.hex**". The editor window then looks like this:

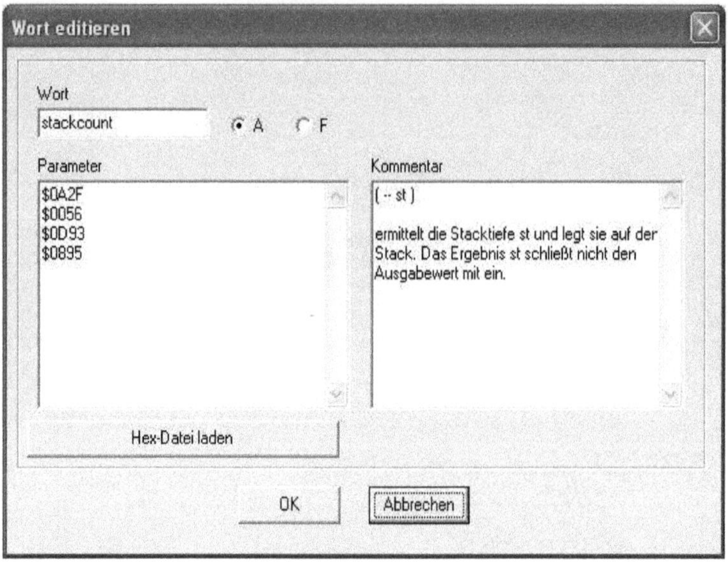

Translation:

Word   A-word or F-word
Parameter   Comment
Load HEX file

                OK   Discard

Figure 24: A and F Words – Parameters added

Now we confirm the entry with the OK button. This completes the generation of our new A-word. However, it is only in the temporary vocabulary. To save it permanently, we finally click on the diskette button in the navigation bar.

Using **stackcount**, we can now easily write the word **stack2com**, which outputs the stack contents via the COM interface:

```
: Stack2com initcom stackcount
          1 do I 95 + sram> >com
          250 waitms loop  ;
```

What is exactly happening here?
First, the COM interface is initialized;

Then the stack depth is determined and placed on the stack as well. Together with the following number 1, it forms the end value and start value of the following **do loop**.

Within this loop, the number 95 is added to the loop index; The result is the address of the respective stack memeory in the SRAM.

The contents of this memory is then placed on the stack via the command **sram>** and passed via **>com** to the serial interface. A short **wait** – although not needed as long as specified here – is required to wait for the COM transmission of one byte to be finished, before starting the translission of the next byte.
For testing, we use the following **main** word:

```
: Main 11 22 33 44 55 66 77 88 99
        Stack2com  ;
```

This places the numbers 11, 22 to 99 on the stack, and immediately afterwards outputs them via **stack2com**. We can easily check this by activating the Terminal program in the Uploader function.

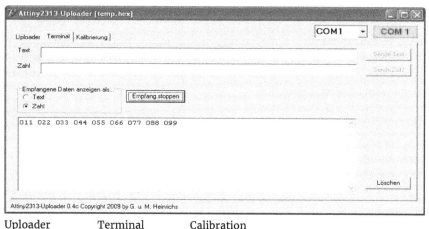

Uploader   Terminal   Calibration
Text
Number
Display received data as ...   Stop receiving data
Text
Number

Picture 25: Uploader window

12 Recursion with MikroForth

The simple concept of our FORTH compiler means, that a Forth word can not call itself directly. For example if we try to interpret the following program

```
: rektest  1 . rectest  ;
: main       rektest  ;
```

The message is generated:

Error: The word "rektest" was not found in the vocabulary
"rektest" has not been entered into the vocabulary!
Warning: Interpreting process aborted ...

However, we can exploit our knowledge of the way how MikroForth works, in order to use a trick to achieve the recursion. For this, we call from the colon definition of **rektest** not the word **rectest** itself, but a different word **zu_rektest**, which on its own part ensures that rectest is executed.

Unfortunately, the word **zu_rektest** cannot call this word as usual, as this would only result in the same error message as above.
How can this call of rektest be implemented differently? For this purpose, we use the fact, that the address of the word to be executed next is waiting on the return stack. The word **zu_rektest** therefore has to do nothing else than just put the address of **rectest** onto the return stack.

A concrete example will explain this approach. The numbers from 1 to 32 are to be output, first counting forward and then counting backwards.

```
: zu_rectest 0 122 >r >r  ;
: rektest    dup dup . 255 waitms  1 + dup
             32 equal skipIf
             zu_rectest  255 waitms  ;
: main  1 rect .  ;
```

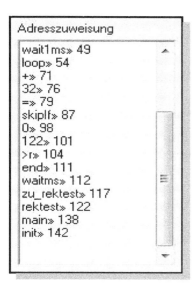

Picture 26: Address allocation

The word **zu_rektest** places the address of **rektest** onto the return stack. This address consists of the high byte **0** and the low byte **122**. How to get to this address? To do this, you only need to look at the address allocation table after compilation. The third-last line in **Picture 26**.

1t shows that the address searched for is **122**. For this address determination, it is not the same which values have been used for the two address bytes in the definition of **zu_rektest**. A subsequent check using the found address is therefore recommended.

The recursion depth is limited by the size of the SRAM.

13 Interrupts

MikroForth also supports the interrupt concept of the ATtiny microcontroller. However, there are only words for the interrupts **INT0**, **INT1** and **T0OVF** (Timer / Couter0 Overflow) defined in the standard vocabulary. However, there is nothing stopping you to extend the vocabulary for other interrupts.

The example of the **INT0** interrupt is now used to explain how interrupt programming is performed in MikroForth. For fundamental questions regarding the interrupt concept, please refer to the relevant chapter.

And this is what our program should do: A Beeper connected to Port D.6 is supposed send out sound contuously. An LED connected to Port B.0 and should be switched via **Ta0** on the falling edge; Whether or not this LED is switched on or off via this push-button, will be determined by the state of **Ta1**.

As usual, the INT0 interrupt must first be initialized. This is done by the word initInt0:

```
initInt0     (f -  )
```

The value of **f** decides, whether the interrupt is generated by a falling (f = 0) or rising edge (f = 1) on the INT0 input (port D.2).

The initialization with **initInt0** also performs the following actions:

- **Configure Port D.2 as input,**
- **Set Port D.2 to high,**
- **Allow interrupts.**

In our case, **f** must be 0, since by pressing Ta0, D.2 changes from high to low.

If the INT0 interrupt is triggered, the word **int0** is now automatically executed. The function of this word is fixed. However, the word body can be programmed as desired by the user; it is imporant that the following form must be followed:

```
: int0 pushreg <custom defined part>
       popreg reti  ;
```

This is, because the interrupt can happen at any time during program execution, and it will usually be executed in the middle of another word. To ensure that the register contents of registers r16-r29 which other word possibly use are not lost, they are all saved first by the word **pushreg**. For this purpose, **pushreg** copies its contents into the registers r2 to r15, which cannot be used for the A-words.

Within the custom section of **int0**, all words can now be used as desired. At the end of this routine, **popreg** restores all registers r16 to r29; Any word interrupted in its execution can now work properly.

When triggering the interrupt, the ATtiny is blocked globally for further interrupts. To re-enable it for interrupts again, the definition of **int0** must be end with the word **reti**. In our case, the definition of the word int0 is as follows:

```
 : int0 pushreg Ta1? . popreg  reti ;
```

The user defined part is very short here: Via **Ta1?** the state of the button **Ta1** is interrogated. If **Ta1** is pressed, a **0** is placed onto the stack and thisd value then output to Port B; otherwise a **1** is placed on the stack and then output. The LED is thus switched on or off, depending on whether or not Ta1 is pushed.
The complete program now looks like this:

```
: int0   pushreg  Ta1? . popreg reti  ;
: beeperAnAus     6 1 outportD 10 waitms
                  6 0 outPortD 10 waitms  ;
: main            6 1 DDBitD 0 initInt0
                  begin BeeperAnAus 0 until  ;
```

In the **main** program, an endless loop is used to generate a rectangular wave with the period duration 2 * 10 ms at Port D.6.

Task:
Test the program; Press the button **Ta0** several times for different button states of **Ta1**. Then delete the reti command and run the test again.

14 Setting-up MikroForth

MikroForth allows the following adjustments:

    1. Program to Upload
    2. Warning hint when overwriting existing words
    3. Selection of the separator in the address allocation table
    4. Display of addresses in HEX or decimal format

The corresponding settings are stored in the file **forth2.ini**.

They can be modified there if needed using an editor.

Program for Uploading
If the program "**Uploader.exe**" is to be used, then the entry in the ini file simply consists of a minus sign:

    externuploader=-

Otherwise, the name of the desired program, along with the full path is specified after the equals sign instead of the minus sign.

Warning when Overwriting Words
Frequently, some words of the current vocabulary must be overwritten with the same word but other functionality.
If the entry is

Ueberschreiben=1   overwrite=1

then MikroForth displays the corresponding warning in a message window. You then have the option to prevent overwriting or continue. If you write the value 0 behind the equals sign, then only a note is displayed in the status area and the old word is overwritten.
You can also change this parameter via Edit Settings.

Selection of the Separator in the Address Allocation Table

In the address assignment table, a so-called separator is located between the Forth word and the corresponding address. By default, this is a double larger character >> with the ASCII code of 187.

You can change this character in the line

separator=187

Enter a different code after the equals sign. However, this code must not be part of a character that is used in the name of an Forth word. Therefore, it is recommended to use only ASCII codes above 127.

Display the Addresses in HEX or Decimal Format

You can define to display the addresses in hex or decimal format.
To do this, the line

hexadressen=1

is used. For entry 1, the addresses are displayed in HEX format; entry 0 changes this to decimal notation.

You can also change this parameter via Edit Settings.

15 Forth Vocabulary

A: Assembler Word   **F:** Forth Word   **C:** Compiler Word   **Status: 01.11.2012**

Word	Type	Comment	Stack
.	A	Sends TOS to Port B; Data Direction Bits of Port B are all set to 1 (OUTPUT)	(n –)
-	A	Res = a – b TOS is subtracted from TOS-1	(a b – res)
/	A	Divides a by b res = a/b (no remainder), remainder is TOS	(a b – res rem)
:	C	: starts the definition of a new Forth Word	
;	C	; ends the definition of this new word	
<	A	a b < a larger than b ? puts 1 (TRUE) flag onto the stack if a < b ist, else the flag 0 onto the stack.	(a b – flag)
>	F	a b > puts 1 (TRUE) onto the stack if a > b ist, else 0.	(a b – flag)
>com	A	sends TOS to the serial COM Interface. BUT: before, the COM Interface has to be initialized using INITCOM.	(n –)

>eprom	A	Writes the value w to address a of the EEPROM. . See as well eprom>	(w a –)
>R	A	Moves the top of stack TOS to the Return Stack See as well R>	(a –)
>sram	A	Saves the value w into a RAM cell at address a	(w a –)
1 bis 255	AC	Transfers the number onto the stack.	(– n)
and	A	res = a and b	(a b – res)

Word	Type	Comment	Stack
begin ... until	A	begin Bef1 Bef2 ... Befn until repeats the instructions Bef1, Bef2, ..., Befn, until the word until reads TOS = 1 flag. begin until	(–) (n –)
blink	F	*bitpattern hp* blink results in *bitpattern* on Port B, waits for *hp* milliseconds, then outputs 0 on Port B and waits again for *hp* millisecons.	(b hp –)
com>	A	Receives a byte via the COM Interface and saves it onto the stack. See as well >com.	(– n)

DDBitB	A	*bit flag* DDBitB sets the relevant bit line of Port B to OUTPUT, if *flag* = 1, else sets it to INPUT.	(bit flag –)
DDBitD	A*	*bit flag* DDBitD sets the relevant bit line of Ports D to |OUTPUT, if *flag* = 1, else sets bit to INPUT.	(bit flag –)
DDRB	A	Writes b into Data Direction Register of Port B.	(b –)
DDRD	A*	Writes d into Data Direction Register of Port D.	(d –)
do ... loop	A	*e a* do Bef1 Bef2 ... Befn loop repeats the instructions Bef1, Bef2, ..., Befn; The loop starts with the index a and runs until value e (included) This loop runs at least once. Within the loop, the program can check the current value via I. do loop	(e a –) (–)
drop	A	Discards the TOS value	(n –)
dup	A	Duplicates the TOS value	(n – n n)

Word	Type	Comment	Stack
end	A	Executes an endless loop and is suggested as last instruction at the end of a program.	(–)
eprom>	A	Reads the value at the EEPROM address a, and copies the value onto the stack. See as well >eprom	(a – w)

getOSCCAL	A	Puts the value OSCCAL onto the Stack. See as well. SetOSCCAL	(– n)
I	A	Copies the loop index I of a do-loop onto the stack. Only allowed to be executed between do and loop.	(– n)
i2cread	A	Read a value from a Slave Chip; if ACK = 0, then an Acknowledge Signal is sent.	(ACK – value)
i2cstart	A	The Start Signal for an I2C Bus transmission is sent. (SDA changes from 1 to 0; then SCL from 1 to 0)	(–)
i2cstop	A	Initializes the I2C Bus (SCL and SDA set to 1); Data Direction Bits for SDA (PortB.5) and SCL (PortB.7) are set.	(–)
i2cwrite	A	One single Byte is sent to the Slave; the Acknowledge Signal is copied to the Stack.	(value/Addr – ACK)
init	F	This is a System Word, and should not be changed or removed.	
initCom	A	Initializes the COM Interface: Pin 2 D0 = RxD Pin 3 D1 = TxD Baud rate = 9600 8 Bit No parity bit	(–)

Word	Type	Comment	Stack
initInt0	A	*signaltyp* initInt0 configures INT0 (Port D2) as Interrupt Input and sets this Input to High. Dependant on the *signaltyp* value, different Input Signals will trigger an Interrupt: 0: change HIGH to LOW 1: change LOW to HIGH Interrupts are generally allowed.	(signaltyp –)
initInt1	A	Same as initInt0, but related to Input INT1 (Port D3).	(signaltyp –)
initT0ovf	A	typ preset initT0ovf initializes Timer0 Interrupt: typ 0: Stop Timer / deactivate 1: System clock /1 2: System clock /8 3: System clock /64 4: System clock /256 5: System clock /1024 6: ext. Clockt, decending on T0 7: ext. Clock, ascending on T0 Timer Interrupts Timer-are allowed, all other Interrupts are allowed *Preset* value within a Interrupt routine has always to be set again.	(typ preset –)
inPortB	A	*bit* InPortB Reads the relevant INPUT bit of Port B and puts 0/1 onto the stack when Input is High or Low. See DDRB and DDBitB	(bit – flag)

| inPortD | A | *bit* InPortD
Reads the relevant INPUT bit of Port D and puts 0/1 onto the stack when Input is High or Low.
See DDRD and DDBitD | (bit – flag) |

Word	Type	Comment	Stack
int0	F	This word is called when INT0 Interrupt is triggered. Construction of an INT0 word:: : int0 pushreg ... <any words> ... popreg reti; During the execution of the int0 word all other Interrupts are inhibited.	(–)
int1	F	This word is called when the INT1 Interrupt is triggered. This can be freely defined.	(–)
not	F	Replaces *flag* by its logic complement.	(*flag* –)
or	A	res = a or b	(a b – res)
outPortB	A	*bit flag* outPortB sets the Output bit of Port B to High/Low if the *flag* value is 0 / 1. See DDRB and DDBitB	(bit flag –)

outPortD	A	*bit flag* outPortD sets the Output bit of Port D to High/Low if the *flag* value is 0 / 1. See. DDRD and DDBitD	(bit flag –)
over	A	Copies the second stack element onto TOS.	(a b – a b a)
popreg	A	All internal registers r16 to r29 are set	(–)
pushreg	A	All internal registers r16-r29 are saved into (r2 – r15).	(–)
R>	A	Moves the highest element of the Return Stack onto the Parameter Stack. See >R	(– a)
reti	A	Interrupts are allowed	(–)
rot	A	Rotates the top 3 stack values	(a b c – b c a)
sei	A	Same as reti	
setOSCCAL	A	Writes the value n into the OSCCALRegister.	(n –)

Word	Type	Comment	Stack
setTimer0	A	Sets the Preset Value of Timer0 (TCNT0).	(preset –)
skipIf	A	Skips over the next Instruction if TOS equals 1 (TRUE) ist.	(n –)

sram>	A	Reads the value of the SRAM cell at address a and copy value to stack	(a – w)
stackInit	A	A System word, this should not be modified or removed.	
swap	A	SWAP exchanges to two numbers at TOS and TOS-1 of the stack.	(n m – m n)
T0ovf	F	This word is called when the Timer0 Overflow Interrupt is triggered, to build an Interrupt word See int0. Within the T0ovf word, there might be the need to set the Preset value of the Timer using setTimer0.	(–)
Ta0?	F	Puts 1/0 onto the Stack, if Ta0 is open / closed (D2=1/0) PortD.2 is configured automatically.	(– bit)
Ta1?	F	Puts 1/0 onto the Stack, if Ta1 is open / closed (D3=1/0) PortD.3 is configured automatically.	
toggleB	A	Toggles the register of Port B.	(–)

VARIABLE	C	Starts the definition of a Variable. VARIABLE *abc* defines Variable *abc*. As result of this definition, the Compiler reserves a memory location in EEPROM. Next, *abc* puts the address of the relevant memory location onto the stack.	
wait	F	Waits for s seconds.	(s –)
wait1ms	A	Waits for 1 millisecond	(–)
waitms	F	Waits for n ms.	(n –)

Word	Type	Comment	Stack
wdogOff	A	Switches the Watchdog Timer off.	(–)
wdogOn	A	Switches the Watchdog Timer on.	(–)
xor	A	res = a xor b	(a b – res)
=	A	*a b =* puts 1 (TRUE) onto the Stack, if *a = b*, else puts 0 (FALSE).	(a b – flag)
+	A	res = a + b	(a b – res)
*	F	res = a * b	(a b – res)

http://www.g-heinrichs.de/wordpress/index.php/attiny/

Exeter 2018_09_10 v18fp_A5

.0 Wie FORTH entstand

Forth wurde von Charles H. Moore 1969 entwickelt. FORTH weist eine Reihe von Eigentümlichkeiten auf, die es stark von herkömmlichen Programmiersprachen unterscheidet. FORTH stellt i. A. nicht nur eine Entwicklungsumgebung, sondern auch ein Betriebssystem dar.

Diese Eigentümlichkeiten lassen sich gut aus der Entstehungsgeschichte erklären. Moore hatte zur Steuerung des Teleskops einer Sternwarte einen Rechner ohne Software gekauft. Er hatte sich vorgenommen, alle Komponenten selbst zu programmieren, die für eine komfortable Programmierung und den Betrieb des Rechners notwendig sind.

Hierzu gehören ein Betriebssystem, eine Hochsprache und eine Entwicklungsumgebung. All diese Komponenten wurden innerhalb eines einzelnen Programms verwirklicht – dem Forth-System.

Bild 1: Charles H. Moore – der Erfinder von Forth

Moore erzählte später selbst:
Ich entwickelte FORTH im Laufe mehrerer Jahre als eine Schnittstelle zwischen mir und den Computern, die ich programmierte. Die traditionellen Sprachen lieferten nicht die Leistungsfähigkeit, Einfachheit oder Flexibilität, die ich wollte. Ich missachtete viele geltende Weisheiten, um exakt die Fähigkeiten einzubauen, die ein produktiver Programmierer benötigt.
Die allerwichtigste davon ist die Möglichkeit, neue Eigenschaften hinzuzufügen, die später einmal notwendig werden. Als ich zum ersten Mal die Ideen, die ich entwickelt hatte, zu einer Einheit zusammenfasste, arbeitete ich auf einer IBM 1130, einem Computer der "dritten

Generation". Das Ergebnis schien mir so leistungsfähig, dass ich es für eine "Sprache der vierten Computergeneration" hielt. Ich würde sie FOURTH genannt haben, aber die 1130 erlaubte nur eine Kennung mit 5 Buchstaben. So wurde aus FOURTH FORTH, immerhin ein nettes Wortspiel.

(Zitiert nach L. Brodie: FORTH)

(forth = vorwärts)

Beispiel Quelle:
http://computermuseum.informatik.uni-stuttgart.de/dev/ibm1130/ibm1130.html

Bild 2: IBM 1130 – der erste Rechner, auf dem Forth lief

1 Wie MikroForth entstand

Eines Tages kam mein Sohn zu mir – er war gerade 14 Jahre alt – und fragte mich, wie man einen Compiler herstelle. Er würde gerne einen selbst programmieren. Nun hatte ich einmal gelesen, wie man Compiler baut; aber das war schon viele Jahre her und das meiste hatte ich wieder vergessen. Allerdings hatte ich sehr wohl noch in Erinnerung, dass der Compilerbau schon etwas komplexer ist und kaum etwas für einen 14-Jährigen. Und das sagte ich ihm dann auch.

Aber er ließ nicht locker. Einige Monate später – ich arbeitete gerade an einem Konzept für eine Mikrocontroller-Fortbildung – kamen wir auf die Idee, einen Compiler für den Mikrocontroller Attiny 2313 zu programmieren. Als Sprache wählten wir FORTH, nicht zuletzt wegen der einfachen Grundstruktur.

Unser FORTH-Compiler sollte allerdings nicht auf dem Mikrocontroller selbst laufen, sondern auf einem PC: Dieser sollte den FORTH-Code in Maschinencode umsetzen, welcher dann auf dem Attiny hochgeladen werden sollte.

Der Compiler selbst ist relativ einfach, er greift auf eine Datenbank zurück, in der sich eine Sammlung von A-Wörtern (Befehlsfolgen in Maschinencode) und F-Wörtern (Befehlsfolgen in FORTH-Code) befindet. Da es uns hauptsächlich um das Prinzip ging, haben wir auch nicht alle gängigen FORTH-Wörter (Befehle) implementiert, sondern nur einen kleinen Bruchteil.

Es war äußerst lehrreich, derartige Programmschnipsel zu schreiben, und ich kann nur jedem raten, dies einmal selbst zu versuchen. Mikro-FORTH macht dies möglich; denn es ist ein offenes System: Die Datenbank kann nach eigenen Vorstellungen beliebig verändert und erweitert werden. Dies entspricht ja gerade auch der Moore'schen Leitvorstellung.

Faszinierend für uns war insbesondere folgender Umstand: Als wir mit dem Projekt begannen, kannten wir nur einige wesentliche Eigenschaften von FORTH. Später – als das Projekt fast fertig war – haben wir einmal recherchiert, wie FORTH im Original beim Compilieren vorgeht. Und siehe da – wir fanden einige unserer Ideen wieder.

Was die Betrachtung von FORTH leistet

-     Verständnis für einfachen Compiler
-     Verständnis für Assembler und Maschinencode
-     Verständnis und Übung im Umgang mit Stapeln
-     Verständnis mit der Übergabe von Parametern
-     Last – but not least: effizienten Maschinencode

2 Einstieg in MikroForth

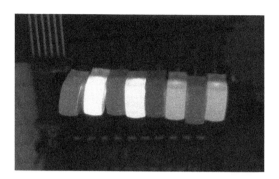

Bild 3: Ergebnisanzeige ueber 8 LEDs

MikroForth ist ein FORTH-Compiler für den Attiny 2313. Damit ist gemeint: Das Programm wird auf einem PC eingegeben und kompiliert. Der dabei erzeugte HEX-Code wird anschließend mit einem Brennprogramm auf den Attiny übertragen.

Im Stile einer Schritt-für-Schritt-Anweisung wollen wir in diesem Kapitel zeigen, wie man mit MikroForth umgeht. Dazu werden wir mit MikroForth den Attiny so programmieren, dass er die Leuchtdioden an Port B in einem solchen Muster wie in **Bild 3** aufleuchten lässt.

Die wenigen benötigten FORTH-Sprachelemente werden wir einfach angeben; wie sie funktionieren - und vor allem: wie man damit eigenständig Programme entwickelt, das werden wir dann in den folgenden Kapiteln darlegen.

Beginnen wir ganz vorne: mit der Installation von MikroForth. Kopieren Sie dazu einfach das Forth-Verzeichnis in das Programme-Verzeichnis (oder auch ein anderes Verzeichnis Ihrer Wahl). Öffnen Sie nun dieses Verzeichnis und starten Sie das Programm Forth2.

Während das Programm startet, lädt es die Datei "forthvoc.vok" mit dem Vorrat an Forth-Befehlen.

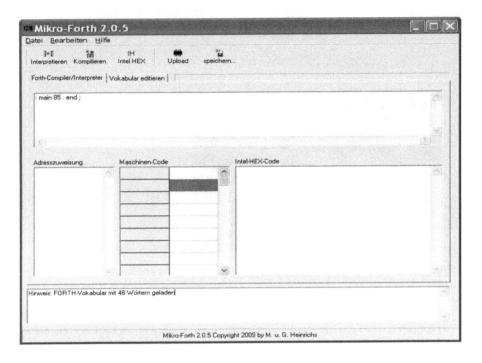

Bild 4: MikroForth Screen

Unser erstes Programm besteht nur aus einer einzigen kurzen Zeile:

```
: main  85  .  end  ;
```

Geben Sie diesen Forth-Quelltext ganz oben im Formular ein (**Bild 4**). Achten Sie auf die Leerzeichen zwischen den einzelnen Befehlen, insbesondere hinter dem Doppelpunkt und vor dem Semikolon; die Eingabe braucht man nicht mit der RETURN-Taste ⊠ abschließen.

Unser Programm gibt zunächst die Zahl 85 am Port B aus; da die Zahl 85 im Zweiersystem als 01010101 geschrieben wird, sollte dies das gewünschte Muster bei den LEDs erzeugen (vgl. **Bild 3**). Anschließend führt das Programm eine Endlosschleife aus.
Als nächstes betätigen wir die "Interpretieren"-Schaltfläche. Wir erhalten die folgende Warnung:

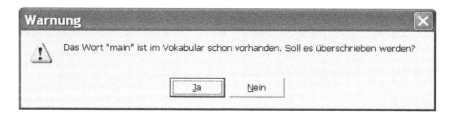

Bild 5: Warnung bezueglich "main" – ueberschreiben oder nicht

Was bedeutet das?
"." oder "end" sind sogenannte Wörter; diese stellen Befehle oder Befehlsfolgen dar, die der Mikrocontroller ausführen soll. Die Gesamtheit aller Wörter bezeichnen wir als Forth-Vokabular. Beim Interpretieren der eingegebenen Zeile wird hier dem Vokabular ein neues Wort "main" hinzugefügt, welches die Zahl 85 und die Wörter "." und "end" zusammenfasst.

Offensichtlich existierte schon ein Wort "main" im Vokabular. Wie wir noch sehen werden, ist dieses Erstellen neuer Befehle ein wesentliches Konzept der Programmiersprache FORTH.

Da das alte "main"-Wort durch unser neues ersetzt werden soll, klicken wir bei dem Warnhinweis in Abb. 3 auf "Ja".

Aus diesem neuen Wort "main" muss nun Maschinencode für den Mikrocontroller erzeugt werden. Dazu betätigen wir die "Kompilieren"-Schaltfläche. Unser FORTH-Compiler besorgt sich aus der Datei "forthvoc.vok" die Programmschnipsel für die einzelnen Bestandteile von "main", also für die Wörter "." und "end" und fügt sie zu einem Gesamtprogramm zusammen.

Im Adresszuweisungsbereich (**Bild 6**) erkennt man die Zuweisung dieser Unterprogramme zu bestimmten Programmspeicheradressen; die Zeile " . ⊠ $001A " bedeutet z.B.: Das Unterprogramm für ".", welches für die Ausgabe auf Port B verantwortlich ist, beginnt bei der Adresse 26 = $1A. Das gesamte Programm wird dann im Maschinencodebereich angezeigt. Unter jeder Adresse finden wir ein Maschinencode-Wort, bestehend aus 2 Byte.

Im Logbuch entdecken wir weitere Einträge; auf deren Bedeutung werden wir zu einem späteren Zeitpunkt eingehen.
So wie es im Maschinencodebereich angezeigt wird, so wird das Programm auch im Mikrocontroller abgelegt (wenn man davon absieht, dass im Speicher des

Mikrocontrollers das höherwertige Byte eines Maschinencode-Wortes nicht wie hier vor, sondern hinter dem niederwertigen steht). Die meisten Brennprogramme benutzen allerdings ein anderes Format, welches noch zusätzliche Kontrollbytes besitzt: das Intel-HEX-Format.

Mit der Schaltfläche "Intel-HEX" wandeln wir deswegen nun unseren Maschinencode in dieses Format um. Der Intel-HEX-Code erscheint sogleich im Intel-HEX-Bereich (**Bild 6**).

Adresszuweisung	Maschinen-Code		Intel-HEX-Code
stackinit» $0014	$0000	$23C0	:1000000023C01895189518951895189518951895652
85» $0017			:10001000189518951895189518951895189518957B
.» $001A	$0001	$1895	:100020001895189518951895A0E6B0E0089505E57F
end» $001F			:100030000D9308951FEF0E9117BB08BB0895FFCFD6
main» $0020	$0002	$1895	:10004000F6DFF8DFFCDF0895EFDFFADFF8DF089571
init» $0024			:00000001FF
	$0003	$1895	
	$0004	$1895	
	$0005	$1895	
	$0006	$1895	
	$0007	$1895	
	$0008	$1895	

Bild 6: Adressenzuweisung, Maschinencode, IntelHEX Code

Zu guter letzt müssen wir den Code noch in den Attiny laden. Bei unserer Attiny-Platine kommt wieder das Uploader-Programm zum Einsatz. Wir rufen es auf, indem wir die "Upload"-Schaltfläche betätigen; der Intel-HEX-Code wird dann automatisch vom Uploader-Programm übernommen und kann auf dem üblichen Weg in den Attiny übertragen werden.

Und wenn Sie keinen Eingabefehler gemacht haben, die LEDs korrekt in die Buchsen gesteckt wurden, die Batterie noch voll ist und die Übertragung reibungslos funktioniert hat, ja - dann sollte auch das Bitmuster aus **Bild 3** tatsächlich angezeigt werden und wir gratulieren Ihnen zur erfolgreichen Implementation Ihres ersten FORTH-Programms!

3 Wörter definieren

Damit ein Mikrocontroller eine bestimmte Aufgabe erfüllt, muss man ihmentsprechende Befehle geben. Bislang hatten wir dazu die Programmiersprache BASCOM oder den Assembler von AVR benutzt. Jetzt soll gezeigt werden, wie man hierzu unser MikroForth-System einsetzen kann.

FORTH-Befehle werden **Wörter** genannt. Derartige Wörter kann man zu Befehlsgruppen zusammenfassen; so entstehen neue Wörter. Die Gesamtheit aller Wörter, welche FORTH zur Verfügung stehen, bezeichnet man als **Vokabular**. Wenn man ein neues Wort herstellt, bedeutet dies letztlich eine Erweiterung des Vokabulars. Am Beispiel eines Ampelprogramms wollen wir dies verdeutlichen. Zur Vereinfachung lassen wir dabei im Folgenden die in Deutschland übliche Rot-Gelb-Phase weg.

```
: ampelzyklus rotphase grünphase gelbphase ;
```

Unser FORTH-Compiler arbeitet grundsätzlich in zwei Schritten. Im ersten Schritt wird der eingegebene Quelltext interpretiert. Der Teil des FORTH-Programms, welcher dafür zuständig ist, wird **Interpreter** genannt. In unserem Fall stößt der Interpreter zunächst auf den Doppelpunkt; dieser zeigt ihm, dass ein neues Wort mit dem Namen ampelzyklus erzeugt werden soll. Dieses Wort setzt sich aus den folgenden Befehlen rotphase, grünphase und gelbphase zusammen. Das Semikolon zeigt dem Interpreter das Ende der Befehlsfolge an.

Da unser Interpreter grundsätzlich nur eine Wortdefinition pro Zeile zulässt, könnte man eigentlich auf das Semikolon verzichten. Andere FORTH-Compiler lassen aber auch mehrere Wortdefinitionen pro Zeile zu; da wird das **Semikolon** als **Begrenzer** unverzichtbar.
Ein neues Wort wird demnach allgemein so definiert:

> **Doppelpunktdefinition**
> : <Name des neuen Wortes> <Befehlsfolge mit bereits definierten Wörtern> ;
> Sämtliche Wörter - auch der Doppelpunkt und das Semikolon - müssen dabei durch (mindestens) ein Leerzeichen getrennt werden.

Testen wir nun unsere erste Wort-Schöpfung: Wir starten das Programm Forth2 und geben den FORTH-Quelltext ein. Groß-Klein-Schreibung spielt für MikroForth übrigens keine Rolle. Anschließend betätigen wir die Interpretieren-Schaltfläche. Im Statusfeld am unteren Rand des Forth2-Formulars erscheinen sogleich die folgenden Meldungen:

```
Fehler: Das Wort "rotphase" wurde im Vokabular nicht gefunden. "ampelzyklus" wurde nicht im Vokabular eingetragen!
Warnung: Interpretiervorgang abgebrochen.
Hinweis: Ggf. existiert noch altes Wort "ampelzyklus" im Vokabular.
```

Bild 7: Fehleranzeige, falls Worte noch nicht definiert waren

Was haben sie zu bedeuten? Die erste Meldung ist eine Fehlermeldung. Fehler führen in der Regel zum Abbruch eines Vorgangs. In diesem Fall weist die nächste Warnung darauf hin, dass der Interpretiervorgang abgebrochen wurde.

Um unseren Fehler beseitigen zu können, müssen wir seine Ursache finden. Offensichtlich kennt unser FORTH-System das Wort rotphase nicht. Das ist nicht schlimm, denn wir können diesen "Fehler" beseitigen, indem wir die Definition von rotphase nachholen. Dazu fügen wir *vor* der Definition von ampelzyklus die folgende Zeile ein:

```
: rotphase rotesLicht an warte rotesLicht aus ;
```

Jetzt beschwert sich unser FORTH-System nicht mehr über das nicht gefundene Wort rotphase, dafür aber meldet es, dass es das Wort rotesLicht nicht finden kann. Also müssen wir auch dieses Wort noch definieren. Ähnliches gilt für die Wörter grünphase, gelbphase, an, warte, aus sowie die Wörter gelbesLicht und grünesLicht.
All diese Definitionen liegen schon fix und fertig in der Datei ampel.frth vor. Öffnen Sie diese Datei mit "Datei - öffnen". Der Quelltext sieht dann so aus:

```
: initialisierePortB 7 DDRB ;
: warte 3 wait ;
: rotesLicht 2 ; : gelbesLicht 1 ;
: grünesLicht 0 ;
: an 1 outPortB ;
: aus 0 outPortB ;
```

```
: rotphase      rotesLicht an warte
                rotesLicht aus ;
: grünphase     grünesLicht an warte
                grünesLicht aus ;
: gelbphase     gelbesLicht an warte
                gelbesLicht aus ;
: ampelzyklus rotphase grünphase
                gelbphase ;
: main initialisierePortB ampelzyklus
                ampelzyklus ;
```

Damit der Interpreter keine Fehler mehr meldet, müssen unsere neuen Wörter - über Zwischenstufen - auf solche Wörter zurückgeführt werden, die sich bereits im Vokabular befinden. In diesem Fall sind das die Zahlen 0, 1, 2, 3 und 7 (Auch diese können als Wörter angesehen werden!) sowie die Wörter wait, DDRB und outPortB.
Das Wort wait veranlasst den Attiny zu warten, outPortB gibt Werte am Port B aus und DDRB stellt das Datenrichtungsregister von PortB ein. Wie diese drei Wörter funktionieren, werden wir in den nächsten Kapiteln noch eingehend betrachten. Hier sollte nur eines deutlich werden:

Komplexe Wörter wie unser Wort ampelzyklus können wir Schritt für Schritt auf elementare Wörter zurückführen; diese Vorgehensweise nennt man auch **Top-Down-Programmierung.**

Wir hätten natürlich auch genau umgekehrt vorgehen können: Ausgehend von den elementaren Wörtern hätten wir immer komplexere Wörter definieren können, bis wir schließlich bei unserem Wort ampelzyklus ausgekommen wären. Diese Vorgehensweise bezeichnet man als **Bottom-Up-Programmierung.** In der Praxis arbeitet man häufig mit beiden Methoden gleichzeitig.

Wichtig ist allerdings für uns: Wörter, die zum Definieren eines neuen Wortes benutzt werden, müssen vorher bereits definiert worden sein. Das bedeutet: Sie müssen schon zum Grundvokabular von FORTH gehören oder in den vorangehenden Zeilen definiert und somit beim Interpretieren bereits zum Vokabular hinzugefügt worden sein. Die grundlegenden Worte müssen im FORTH-Quellcode also immer oben stehen, die daraus abgeleiteten weiter unten.

Unabhängig davon, ob wir die Top-Down-Methode oder die Bottom-Up-Methode benutzen - im Ergebnis ist das zu lösende Problem, eine Ampelanlage zu programmieren, schrittweise in viele kleine Teilprobleme zerlegt worden. Solche

Teilprobleme nennt man auch **Module** und die Zerlegung selbst wird als **Modularisierung** bezeichnet. Modularisierung ist ein wesentliches Merkmal der Programmiersprache FORTH.

Gute FORTH-Programme zeichnen sich dadurch aus, dass die einzelnen Wort-Definitionen sinnvolle Einheiten bilden und nicht zu lang sind. Natürlich sollten auch die benutzten Wortnamen aussagekräftig sein.

Schauen wir daraufhin noch einmal den Quelltext an. Erfüllt er die Kriterien eines guten FORTH-Codes? Sicherlich sind die ersten Zeilen - so kurz sie auch sein mögen - nicht unmittelbar einleuchtend; das hängt aber damit zusammen, dass wir die Wörter wait, DDRB und outPortB noch nicht genügend kennen. Wort-Folgen wie

```
grünesLicht an warte grünesLicht aus
```

lassen sich dagegen auch ohne Programmierkenntnisse leicht verstehen.

Das wichtigste Wort im ganzen Quelltext haben wir noch nicht besprochen; es ist das Wort main. Wenn der Attiny eingeschaltet wird, startet er immer mit der Ausführung genau dieses Wortes. Das Wort **main** hat demnach die Bedeutung eines Hauptprogramms; daher stammt auch die Wahl des Wortnamens ("main" = "haupt"). Alle Aktionen, welche der Mikrocontroller ausführen soll, müssen letztlich von diesem Wort ausgehen.

Somit muss der Quelltext immer mit der Definition von main enden, und beim Interpretieren muss man das Überschreiben eines bereits bestehenden main-Wortes stets zulassen; ansonsten arbeitet FORTH mit einem solchen alten "Hauptprogramm". Und das hat womöglich gar nichts mit unserer Ampelsteuerung zu tun.
In unserem Fall sehen wir als letzte Zeile:

```
: main initPortB ampelzyklus ampelzyklus ;
```

Das bedeutet: Der Attiny soll zunächst das Port B initialisieren und danach zwei volle Ampelzyklen durchlaufen.

Bestimmt haben Sie inzwischen der Versuchung nicht mehr widerstehen können und den Quelltext unseres vollständigen Ampelprogramms interpretieren lassen. Wenn Sie ihn nicht abgeändert haben, müsste im Statusfeld jetzt angezeigt werden, dass das (im Vokabular schon) bestehende Wort main (wie gewünscht) überschrieben wurde.

Der für uns aufwändige Teil des Programmierens ist damit getan. Der Quelltext wurde erstellt und die neu definierten Wörter ins Vokabular übernommen. Jetzt muss unser FORTH-System ans Arbeiten: Die Wörter müssen in Attiny-Maschinencode umgesetzt werden. Diesen Schritt bezeichnet man als **Kompilieren**. Wie dieses Kompilieren im Einzelnen funktioniert, lässt sich bei FORTH recht gut nachvollziehen. In einem späteren Kapitel werden wir darauf ausführlich eingehen.

Jetzt aber machen wir es uns einfach: Wir drücken die Kompilieren-Schaltfläche und im Anschluss daran die Intel-HEX-Code-Schaltfläche. Den HEX-Code übertragen wir schließlich wie üblich mit dem Uploader-Programm auf den Attiny, auf dessen Platine wir in weiser Voraussicht eine rote LED bei PortB.2, eine gelbe bei PortB.1 und eine grüne bei PortB.0 eingesteckt haben.

Probieren Sie es selbst aus. Bestimmt werden auch Sie bei Ihrer Attiny-Platine die zwei Ampelzyklen beobachten können.

Aufgabe 1:
Ergänzen Sie die Datei ampel.frth so, dass eine "deutsche Ampel" mit einer zusätzlichen GelbGrün-Phase entsteht.

4 Arbeiten mit dem Stack

Der Stack ist einer der wichtigsten Konzepte von FORTH. Wir können uns den **Stack** vorstellen als einen Stapel von Zahlen. In der Tat heißt das englische Wort "stack" auf deutsch nichts anderes als **Stapel**. Wozu dient nun der Stack und wie wird er praktisch eingesetzt? Das soll in diesem Kapitel erklärt werden.

Schauen wir uns zunächst das Wort stapeln an:

```
: stapeln 11 22 33 44 55 ;
```

Wird dieses Wort ausgeführt, so werden die Zahlen 11, 22, 33, 44 und 55 der Reihe nach auf den Stack gelegt. Anschaulich können wir uns das so vorstellen:

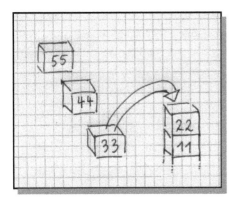
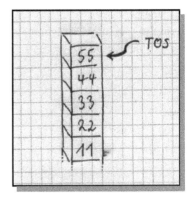

Bild 8: Zahlen auf den Stapel gelegt   **Bild 9:** Resultat mit Top Of Stack (TOS)

Am Ende liegen unsere fünf Zahlen übereinander, die 11 zuunterst, die 55 ganz oben. Die oberste Zahl wird auch **TOS** (= Top Of Stack) genannt.

Wörter wie z. B. "." und wait greifen auf diesen Stapel zu. Das Wort "." holt sich z. B. den TOS vom Stapel und gibt diese Zahl auf dem Port B aus; das Wort wait greift sich auch den TOS und wartet entsprechend viele Sekunden. Wird das folgende Wort

```
: ausgabe . wait . ;
```

nach dem Wort stapeln ausgeführt, geschieht folgendes: "." holt die Zahl 55 vom Stack und gibt sie auf Port B aus.

wait holt die Zahl 44 vom Stack und wartet entsprechend viele Sekunden.
"." holt die Zahl 33 vom Stack und gibt sie auf Port B aus.
Am Schluss befinden sich nur noch die Zahlen 11 und 22 auf dem Stack.

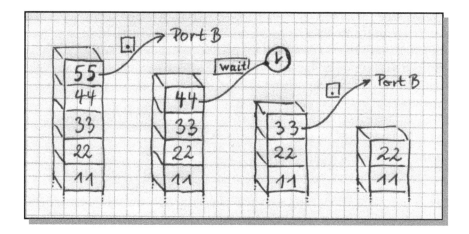

Bild 10: Werte von Stack nehmen und ausfuehren

Wörter verändern i. A. den Stack: Unser Wort stapeln legt 5 Zahlen auf den Stack, unser Wort ausgabe entfernt die obersten drei Zahlen. Manche Worte holen erst Zahlen vom Stapel und legen anschließend neue Werte auf dem Stapel ab. Dies gilt insbesondere auch für Rechenoperationen wie Plus und Minus.

Wir schauen uns einmal etwas genauer an, wie man mithilfe des Wortes "+" in FORTH zwei Zahlen addiert. Zum Beispiel sollen die Zahlen 4 und 9 addiert werden. Von den meisten Taschenrechnern, aber auch von vielen Programmiersprachen, ist man es gewohnt, die folgende Anweisung zu schreiben:

4 + 9

Das Rechenzeichen steht zwischen den beiden Summanden; man spricht hier von einer **Infix**Schreibweise.
In FORTH schreibt man dies so:

4 9 +   (Leerzeichen zwischen 4 und 9 nicht vergessen!)

Hier werden zuerst die beiden Summanden eingegeben und anschließend erst das Rechenzeichen; man spricht hier von einer **Postfix**-Schreibweise.

Was steckt dahinter? Natürlich unser Stapel! Zunächst werden die Zahlen 4 und 9 auf den Stapel gelegt; dann holt das Wort "+" diese beiden Zahlen vom Stapel, addiert sie und legt das Ergebnis (also 13) wieder auf den Stapel.

Der Vorteil dabei: Das Wort "+" führt bei FORTH die Addition sofort aus; beide Summanden liegen ja bereits vor. Bei der Infix-Schreibweise ist das nicht so einfach möglich. Hier müssen sich Taschenrechner oder Computer das Pluszeichen zunächst merken; die eigentliche Addition kann erst ausgeführt werden, wenn nach dem zweiten Summanden noch ein weiterer Befehl z. B. in Form von "=" erfolgt.

Wenden wir unsere Kenntnisse nun an, um den Attiny mit FORTH die Rechenaufgabe 4 + 9 durchführen zu lassen. Unser Programm sieht so aus:

```
: main 4 9 + . ;
```

Wir geben es in das Quelltext-Feld ein, interpretieren, kompilieren und übertragen es. Die Leuchtdioden am Port B zeigen tatsächlich die Zahl 13 an (&B00001101).

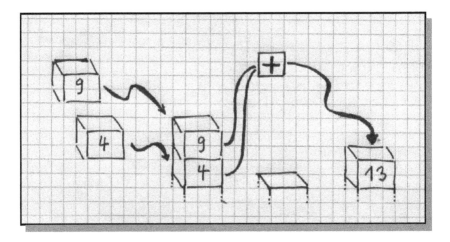

Bild 11: 4 auf den Stack, 9 auf den Stack, addieren und Resultat wieder auf den Stack

Wir haben bereits gelernt, was hier im Einzelnen geschieht: Zuerst werden die Zahlen 4 und 9 auf den Stack gelegt; dann holt das Wort "+" diese beiden Zahlen vom Stack, addiert sie und legt das Ergebnis wieder auf den Stack. Das nächste Wort "." holt sich diese Zahl 13 vom Stack und gibt sie auf dem Port B aus.

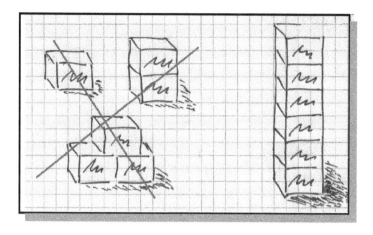

Bild 12: Bei Forth sind alle Arbeits-Daten auf dem Stack gespeichert – nicht in verschiedenen Bereichen

Wir sehen: Der Stack ist eine Art Marktplatz, auf dem die einzelnen Wörter Zahlen holen oder auch abgeben können. Im Gegensatz zu einem echten Marktplatz können hier allerdings nur Zahlen gehandelt werden; außerdem gibt es hier nur einen einzigen Stand und an diesem Stand liegen die Zahlen nicht irgendwie nebeneinander, sondern ordentlich übereinander auf einem einzigen Stapel.

An dieser Stelle sei schon verraten: FORTH stellt noch weitere Möglichkeiten zum Austausch von Daten zwischen den Wörtern zur Verfügung, z. B. sogenannte Variablen. Der Austausch über den Stack ist aber die wichtigste Methode. Deswegen wollen wir den Umgang mit dem Stack noch etwas üben.
Wie man einfache Rechenaufgaben mit FORTH lösen kann, haben wir schon kennen gelernt. Wie aber sieht es mit komplexen Termen aus?

1. Beispiel:
```
    Term:      ( 3 + 5 ) * 2
    FORTH:     3 5 + 2 *
```
2. Beispiel:
```
    Term:      120 - 5 * 20
    FORTH:     120 5 20 * -
```

Bei dem letzten Beispiel könnten die Zahlen 120, 5 und 20 schon fertig auf dem Stack liegen; um das Ergebnis des Terms zu erhalten, müssten nur noch die Worte "*" und "-" hintereinander ausgeführt werden.

Ginge das auch beim ersten Beispiel? Nein, auf keinen Fall wäre das so einfach wie im Beispiel 2: Da die Zahl 2 auf dem TOS liegt, würde jede Operation sich auf jeden Fall (auch) auf diese Zahl 2 beziehen. Die Klammern im Term verlangen aber, dass zunächst die Zahlen 3 und 5 verarbeitet (addiert) werden.

Es gibt aber eine Reihe von FORTH-Wörtern, die die Zahlen auf dem Stack manipulieren (vertauschen, entfernen oder verdoppeln) können:

5 Port-Befehle

MikroForth stellt folgende Port-Befehle zur Verfügung:

Wort	Typ	Kommentar	Stack
.	A	gibt TOS auf Port B aus; (Datenrichtungsbits von Port B werden zuvor alle auf 1 gesetzt.)	(n –)
blink	F	b hp blink gibt das Bitmuster von b auf Port B aus, wartet hp Millisekunden, gibt 0 auf Port B aus und wartet wieder hp Millisekunden.	(b hp –)
DDBitB	A	bit flag DDBitB setzt den Anschluss bit des Ports B als Ausgang, wenn flag = 1, sonst als Eingang.	(bit flag –)
DDBitD	A	bit flag DDBitD setzt den Anschluss bit des Ports D als Ausgang, wenn flag = 1, sonst als Eingang.	(bit flag –)
DDRB	A	schreibt b in das Datenrichtungs-register des Ports B.	(b –)
DDRD	A	schreibt d in das Datenrichtungs-register des Ports D.	(d –)

Wort	Typ	Kommentar	Stack
InPort B	A	bit InPortB liest den Eingang bit des Ports B und legt 1/0 auf den Stack, wenn er high/low ist. Vgl. DDRB und DDBitB	(bit – flag)
InPort D	A	bit InPortD liest den Eingang bit des Ports D und legt 1/0 auf den Stack, wenn er high/low ist. Vgl. DDRD und DDBitD	(bit – flag)
Wort	**Typ**	**Kommentar**	**Stack**
outPort B	A	bit flag outPortB setzt den Ausgang bit des Ports B auf high/low, wenn flag = 1/0 ist. Vgl. DDRB und DDBitB	(bit flag –)
outPort D	A	bit flag outPortD setzt den Ausgang bit des Ports D auf high/low, wenn flag = 1/0 ist. Vgl. DDRD und DDBitD	(bit flag –)
Ta0?	F	Legt 1/0 auf Stack, wenn Taster Ta0 offen/geschlossen (D2=1/0) PortD.2 wird automatisch konfiguriert.	(– bit)
Ta1?	F	Legt 1/0 auf Stack, wenn Taster Ta1 offen/geschlossen (D3=1/0) PortD.3 wird automatisch konfiguriert.	

Exemplarisch werden wir hier die Wörter ".", **blink**, **Ta0?**, **DDBitD**, **OutPortD** und **InPortD** behandeln. Die restlichen Wörter sind in ihrer Bedeutung ganz ähnlich.

Um etwas interessantere Beispiele verwenden zu können, wollen wir allerdings zuvor eine einfache FORTH-Schleifenkonstruktion vorstellen: die BEGIN-UNTIL-Schleife. Diese sieht folgendermaßen aus:

begin Bef1 Bef2 Bef3 ... **until**

Die Befehle Bef1, Bef2, Bef3, ... werden der Reihe nach immer wieder durchlaufen. Allerdings geschieht dies nur solange, wie das Wort until auf demTOS eine 0 vorfindet. Genauer gesagt: Das Wort until holt den Wert aus dem TOS und kontrolliert nach, ob er 0 oder 1 ist. Ist er 0 (FALSE), wird die Schleife ein weiteres Mal ausgeführt; ist er 1 (TRUE), so wird die Schleife beendet. Schreibt man also unmittelbar vor das Wort until eine 0, so wird eine Endlosschleife gebildet:

```
: endlos Bef1 Bef2 Bef3 ... 0 until ;
```

Kommen wir zu unserem ersten Beispiel: Alle LEDs an Port B sollen im Abstand von 100 ms immer wieder an- und ausgehen. Das Programm dafür ist recht einfach:

```
: main begin 255 . 100 waitms 0 . 100
       waitms 0 until ;
```

Schauen wir uns die Definition von main Wort für Wort an. begin leitet die Endlosschleife ein, welche durch 0 until begrenzt wird. Innerhalb der Schleife wird zuerst 255 auf den Stack gelegt. Diese Zahl wird durch das Wort ".". sogleich vom Stapel genommen und am Port B ausgegeben. Dabei wird durch "." Port B automatisch als Ausgang konfiguriert; d. h. DDRB wird auf &B11111111 gesetzt.

Nun sind also alle LEDs an Port B eingeschaltet. Danach wird die Zahl 100 auf den Stack gelegt, um sogleich von dem Wort "waitms" geholt zu werden: Der Mikrocontroller wartet jetzt 100 ms. Anschließend wird die Zahl 0 auf dem Port B ausgegeben; die LEDs werden somit alle ausgeschaltet. Dann wartet der Mikrocontroller abermals 100 ms. Wir sind am Ende eines Schleifendurchlaufs angekommen. Nun beginnt das Ganze wieder von vorne und so weiter und so weiter... Unsere LEDs an Port B blinken also fortwährend.

In unserem zweiten Beispiel soll eine LED an PortD.6 über den Taster Ta0 aus- und eingeschaltet werden. Genauer gesagt soll die LED aus sein, solange der Taster Ta0 gedrückt ist, und leuchten, solange der Taster nicht betätigt ist. Das FORTH-Programm kann durch folgende Zeilen gebildet werden:

```
: schalten begin Ta0? 6 swap
         outPortD 0 until ;
```

```
: vorbereiten 6 1 DDBitD ;
```

```
: main vorbereiten schalten ;
```

Zunächst wird durch das Wort vorbereiten das Bit 6 des Datenrichtungsregisters von D auf 1 gesetzt; Port D.6 wird also als Ausgang konfiguriert. Das Wort schalten besteht aus einer Endlosschleife; zu Beginn der Schleife kontrolliert das Wort Ta0?, ob der Taster Ta0 gedrückt ist oder nicht. Ist Ta0 gedrückt, legt es den Wert 0 auf den Stack, sonst den Wert 1. Ähnlich wie schon bei dem Wort ".", wird der zugehörige Eingang Port D.2 von dem Wort Ta0? automatisch konfiguriert (Eingang und Pull-up).

Anschließend wird die Zahl 6 auf den Stack gelegt; swap tauscht diesen Wert 6 mit dem von Ta0? gelieferten Ein-Aus-Wert aus. Nun liegen der Bit-Wert 6 und der Ein-Aus-Wert genau in der Reihenfolge auf dem Stapel, wie sie von OutPortD benötigt werden: unten der Bit-Wert und oben der An-Aus-Wert (im Vokabular als Flag bezeichnet). 6 1 OutPortD schaltet z. B. die LED an PortD.6 an; 6 0 OutPortD schaltet sie aus.

Beachten Sie: Nur bei den Wörtern ".", Ta0?, Ta1?
und blink erfolgt eine automatische Konfigurierung der Ports;
bei allen anderen Port-Befehlen müssen die Datenrichtungsbytes
bzw. -Bits vom Anwender selbst mithilfe der Wörter
DDRB, DDRD, DDBitB und DDBitD eingestellt werden.

Im dritten Beispiel soll eine Blink-Schleife über den Taster Ta0 abgebrochen werden. Genauer gesagt soll das Bitmuster 01010101 solange ein- und ausgeschaltet werden, bis der Taster Ta0 gedrückt wird. Das zugehörige Programm ist auch wieder sehr kurz und sieht so aus:

```
: main begin 85 100 blink Ta0? not until ;
```

Innerhalb der BEGIN-UNTIL-Schleife wird zunächst das blink-Wort mit dem Bitmuster &B01010101 = 85 und der halben Periodendauer 100 ms ausgeführt. Anschließend wird mit Ta0? der Zustand des Tasters Ta0 abgefragt; ist dieser Taster gedrückt, wird eine 0 auf den Stapel gelegt, sonst eine 1.

Ohne das folgende Wort **not** würde dieser Ein-Aus-Wert des Tasters direkt von **until** ausgewertet: der Zustandswert 0 (Taster gedrückt) würde zu einem weiteren Schleifendurchlauf führen und der Zustandswert 1 (Taster offen) würde die Schleife abbrechen. Die Schleife würde also durch ein Öffnen und nicht - wie gefordert - durch ein Schließen des Tasters beendet.

Um zu einem korrekt funktionierenden Programm zu gelangen, muss also der Zustandswert umgekehrt werden: Aus dem Wert 1 muss eine 0 und aus dem Zustandswert 0 muss eine 1 gemacht werden. Dies kann man mit dem Wort not erreichen: Dieses Wort holt den Zustandswert vom Stapel und ersetzt ihn durch sein logisches Komplement. Die Wortfolge Ta0? not liefert jetzt wie gewünscht auf dem TOS den Wert 0, wenn der Taster offen ist, und den Wert 1, wenn der Taster geschlossen ist.

Aufgabe 1:
Ein Blick in den FORTH-Editor zeigt, wie das Wort Ta0? definiert ist.

```
: Ta0? 2 0 DDBitD 2 1 outPortD 2 InPortD ;
```

Erläutern Sie diese Definition.

Aufgabe 2
Wie ließe sich das Programm zum ersten Beispiel mithilfe des blink-Wortes vereinfachen?

Aufgabe 3
Ändern Sie das Programm des zweiten Beispiels so ab, dass die LED leuchtet, wenn der Taster gedrückt ist, und sonst nicht.

Aufgabe 4
Der Attiny soll die Anzahl der Tastendrücke beim Taster Ta0 an PortB anzeigen; PortB muss entsprechend mit 8 LED bestückt werden. Beachten Sie: Der Tastendruck dauert immer eine gewisse Zeit; selbst bei flotten Menschen bleibt der Taster für mehrere Millisekunden geschlossen, für den Attiny ist das aber eine halbe Ewigkeit!

6 Schleifen und Verzweigungen

Einen ersten Schleifentyp haben Sie im Kapitel über die Portbefehle schon kennen gelernt, die BEGIN-UNTIL-Schleife. Sie hat folgende Form:

begin Bef1 Bef2 Bef3 ... **until**

Durch diese Konstruktion wird die Befehlsfolge zwischen begin und until solange ausgeführt, bis das Wort until auf dem TOS eine 1 vorfindet. 1 wird allgemein als Wahrheitswert TRUE interpretiert, 0 als FALSE.

Die Schleife wird also solange ausgeführt, bis auf dem Stack der Wahrheitswert TRUE vorliegt. Zu beachten ist, dass until den Wert auch aus dem TOS holt; es muss also bei jedem Schleifendurchlauf dafür gesorgt werden, dass für das Wort until ein passender Wahrheitswert auf den Stack gelegt wird.

Da im Kapitel über die Portbefehle schon einige praktische Beispiele für die BEGIN-UNTIL-Schleife vorgestellt worden sind, wollen wir uns gleich dem nächsten Schleifentyp zuwenden, der Zählschleife. In FORTH sieht sie folgendermaßen aus:

ew sw do Bef1 Bef2 Bef3 ... loop

Die Bezeichner ew (Endwert) und sw (Startwert) stehen hier für den Wert des Schleifenindex beim letzten bzw. ersten Schleifendurchlauf. Innerhalb der Zählschleife, also zwischen den Wörtern do und loop, kann man auf den Schleifenindex mithilfe des Wortes I zurückgreifen: I legt den aktuellen Schleifenindex auf den Stapel. Schauen wir uns ein einfaches Beispiel dazu an:

```
: zählen 25 10 do I . 100 waitms loop ;
```

Bei diesem Wort startet die Zählschleife mit dem Index 10. Diese Zahl wird zunächst durch das Wort I auf den Stapel gelegt und mit dem Wort . am Port B ausgegeben. Nach 100 Millisekunden Wartezeit wird der Schleifenindex automatisch erhöht und die Schleife ein weiters mal durchlaufen. Die Schleife wird ein letztes Mal durchlaufen, wenn der Schleifenindex den Wert 25 hat. Unser Programmzählt also im Zehntelsekunden-Rhythmus von 10 bis 25 und hört dann auf.

Man beachte bei der Angabe der Werte für den Schleifenindex die Reihenfolge: Zuerst wird der Endwert und dann der Startwert angegeben.

Als weiteres Beispiel schauen wir uns die FORTH-Definition der Multiplikation an:

```
: * 0 swap 1 do swap dup rot + loop ;
```

Lautet das Hauptprogramm z. B.

```
: main 12 7 * . ;
```

so wird die Zahl 12 insgesamt 7 mal zur 0 addiert; die Multiplikation wird also auf eine Mehrfachaddition zurückgeführt. Wie das im Detail abläuft, sollte der Leser einmal selbst überlegen, indem er für jeden einzelnen Schritt den Inhalt des Stacks notiert. Unser MikroForth besitzt nur einen einzigen Verzweigungstyp, die skipIf-Anweisung. Dieses Wort wertet zunächst den TOS aus; liegt auf dem TOS der Wert 1 (TRUE), wird die nächste Anweisung übersprungen. Liegt auf dem TOS der Wert 0 (FALSE), wird einfach mit dem nächsten Befehl (Wort) weitergearbeitet.

```
1 skipIf Bef1 Bef2 Bef3 ...
```

Hier wird nach dem Wort skipIf das Wort Bef1 übersprungen und sofort mit demWort Bef2 weitergearbeitet.

Es folgt das Wort Bef3 usw.

```
0 skipIf Bef1 Bef2 Bef3 ...
```

Hier wird nach dem Wort skipIf mit dem Wort Bef1 weitergearbeitet. Es folgen die Worte Bef2 und Bef3 usw.

Häufig ergeben sich dabei die Wahrheitswerte 0 und 1 als Ergebnisse von Vergleichen. Hier kommen Vergleichsoperatoren zum Einsatz. Ähnlich wie die Rechenoperatoren +, *, - und / werden sie bei FORTH auch in der Postfix-Schreibweise benutzt. Durch

```
7 2 >
```

wird also überprüft, ob 7 > 2 gilt. Da das in diesem Fall wahr ist, wird als Ergebnis dieser Vergleichsoperation der Wert 1 (TRUE) auf den Stapel gelegt. Weitere Vergleichsoperatoren sind < und =.

Ein Beispiel soll erläutern, wie Vergleichsoperatoren und Verzweigungen sinnvoll eingesetzt werden können. Ein Messprozess möge bereits zwei Messwerte (z. B. Temperaturwerte) auf den Stapel gelegt haben. Das Wort unterschied soll - wie der Name schon sagt - den Unterschied der beiden Zahlen bestimmen; es könnte z. B. erforderlich sein, vom Mikrocontroller bestimmte Maßnahmen einleiten zu lassen, wenn dieser Unterschied zu groß ist.

Kümmern wir uns zunächst um Berechnung und Ausgabe des Unterschieds. Auf den ersten Blick scheint dieses Problem recht einfach zu lösen zu sein:

```
: unterschied - . ;
```

Zu Testzwecken geben wir bei unserem Forth-Compiler ein:

```
: main 7 2 unterschied ;
```

Nach dem Interpretieren, Compilieren und Übertragen zeigt unser Mikrocontroller den Wert 5 an - wie erwartet! Nun geben wir die Messwerte aber einmal in umgekehrter Reihenfolge ein:

```
: main 2 7 unterschied ;
```

Nun zeigt der Mikrocontroller amPort B den Wert 251(!) an. Wie lässt sich dieses offensichtlich unsinnige Ergebnis erklären, und - mindestens genau so wichtig - wie lässt sich unser Programm verbessern?

Zunächst zur Erklärung: Bei der Subtraktion 2 - 7 gelangt der Mikrocontroller in den Bereich unter 0. Er arbeitet dabei wie ein Kilometerzähler: Wenn man ausgehend vom Kilometerstand 0002 nun 7 km rückwärts fährt, kommt man beim Stand von 9995 aus. Der Kilometerstand springt nämlich beim Rückwärtszählen von 0000 auf 9999. Ganz ähnlich arbeitet der Mikrocontroller: Er springt beim Rückwärtszählen von 000 auf 255.

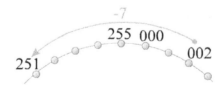

Bild 13: Addieren nach rechts – Subtrahieren nach links

Das Problem liegt also offensichtlich in der Reihenfolge der beiden Messwerte. Um das Programm zu verbessern, müssen wir dafür sorgen, dass die Messwerte ausgetauscht werden, wenn der erste Messwert kleiner als der zweite ist. Hier kann unser skipIf-Wort zum Einsatz kommen; für den zugehörigen Vergleich müssen die Messwerte allerdings vorher noch kopiert werden.

```
: unterschied over over > skipIf swap - . ;
```

Das folgende Stapelbild macht deutlich, was beider Ausführung von unterschied geschieht.

$$a\ b \to a\ b\ a \to a\ b\ a\ b \to a\ b\ \text{flag} \begin{array}{c} \text{flag} = 1 \\ \to a\text{-}b \\ \to b\ a \to b\text{-}a \\ \text{flag} = 0 \end{array} \to Ausgabe$$

Aufgabe 1
Wenn der Unterschied der beiden Messwerte auf dem Stapel größer als 3 ist, dann soll ein Warnton über D.6 und den Beeper ausgegeben werden.

Aufgabe 2
Schreiben Sie eine Definition für das FORTH-Wort "<=".

Aufgabe 3
Wie lautet die FORTH-Definition für das Wort **not** ?

7 Alles unter Kontrolle: COM, I2C und EEPROM

Mikrocontroller werden häufig als Herzstück autonomer Messstationen eingesetzt. Folgende Voraussetzungen sollten sie dazu erfüllen:

1.   Sie müssen einen Speicher besitzen, der die Messdaten sicher verwahren kann - möglichst auch dann noch, wenn die elektrische Versorgung des Mikrocontrollers ausfällt.

2.   Sie müssen gängige Kommunikationsschnittstellen zu Sensoren besitzen.

3.   Sie müssen gängige Kommunikationsschnittstellen zu Terminals besitzen, damit die Daten problemlos zur weiteren Auswertung auf Computer übertragen werden können.

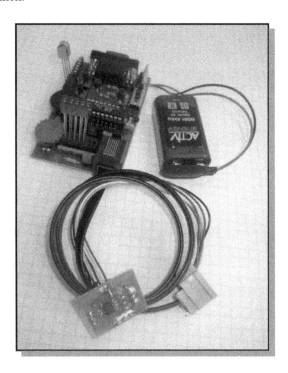

Bild 14: Ein komplettes Projektsystem: das Board mit MikroForth, USBtoTTL Converter und Batterie

All dies kann unser Attiny2313 mit MikroForth leisten:

Er besitzt ein EEPROM, welches Daten auch ohne elektrische Quelle dauerhaft speichern kann.

Über den I²C-Bus kann er mit Sensoren und anderen Geräten kommunizieren und über die COM-Schnittstelle kann er die gespeicherten Daten an ein Terminal senden.

Für genauere Erläuterungen zu EEPROM, I²C und COM-Schnittstelle sei auf die entsprechenden Abschnitte verwiesen. Hier soll anhand eines einfachen Beispiels betrachtet werden, wie MikroForth zum Anfertigen eines Temperaturmessprotokolls eingesetzt werden kann.

Der Aufbau ist einfach: An die I²C-Buchse der Attiny-Platine wird ein Temperatursensor LM75 mit der I²C-Adresse 157 angeschlossen (**Bild 16**).
Nicht vergessen sollten Sie, die Jumper zu setzen, die zum Pull-Up der beiden Leitungen SDA und SCL erforderlich sind. Der Datenaustausch mit dem PC erfolgt über dasselbe Kabel wie die Programmierung.

Folgende FORTH-Wörter stellt MikroForth für EEPROM, I²C und COM zur Verfügung:

Wort	Typ	Kommentar	Stack
>com	A	sendet TOS an die COM-Schnittstelle. Vorher muss die COM-Schnittstelle mit INITCOM initialisiert worden sein.	(n –)
>eprom	A	schreibt den Wert w in die Adresse a des EEPROMs. Vgl. eprom>	(w a –)
Wort	Typ	Kommentar	Stack

com>	A	legt über COM-Schnittstelle empfangenes Byte auf den Stack. Vgl. >com.	(– n)
eprom>	A	liest den Wert w aus der EEPROMAdresse a und legt ihn auf den Stack Vgl. >eprom	(a – w)
i2cread	A	Ein Wert wird vom Slave gelesen; wenn ACK = 0 ist, wird ein Acknowledge-Signal gegeben.	(ACK – Wert)
i2cstart	A	Startsignal für I²C-Bus wird gesendet (SDA von 1 auf 0; dann SCL von 1 auf 0)	(–)
i2cstop	A	initialisiert den I²C-Bus (SCL und SDA auf 1); Datenrichtungsbits für SDA (PortB.5) und SCL (PortB.7) werden gesetzt.	(–)
i2cwrite	A	Ein einzelnes Byte (Wert oder Adresse) wird an den Slave gesendet; das Acknowledge-Bit wird auf den Stack gelegt.	(Wert/Adr – ACK)
initCom	A	initialisiert die COM-Schnittstelle: D0 = RxD D1 = TxD Baudate = 9600 8 Bit kein Paritätsbit	(–)

Zunächst schauen wir uns den Messprozess an: Der Attiny soll im Sekundenabstand 20 Temperaturwerte im EEPROM aufzeichnen. Dies leisten die beiden Wörter messung und main:

```
: messung i2cstop i2cstart 1 wait
         157 i2cwrite 1 i2cread ;
```

```
: main 20 1 do messung I >eprom loop ;
```

Schauen wir uns zunächst die Definition von messung an: Mit i2cstop wird die I²C-Schnittstelle initialisiert (SCL und SDA auf high), mit i2cstart wird das Startsignal gegeben (SDA wechselt von high auf low), mit 157 i2cwrite wird unser Temperatursensor adressiert.

Schließlich wird mit 1 I2cread ein Temperaturwert vom LM75 abgefragt und auf den Stack gelegt; der Parameter 1 sorgt dafür, dass kein Acknowledge-Signal gegeben wird. Ein Acknowledge würde nämlich den LM75 dazu veranlassen, als nächstes die Nachkommastelle zu senden.

Man beachte ferner, dass der LM75 bis zu 300 ms für eine einzige Temperaturmessung benötigt. Eine längere Pause (hier 1 Sekunde) zwischen den einzelnen Messungen ist also unabdingbar!

Das Wort **main** besteht im Wesentlichen aus einer Zählschleife, bei der die einzelnen Messwerte imEEPROM abgelegt werden. Der Schleifenindex I gibt jeweils die Adressnummer des EEPROMs an.

Nun müssen wir die gemessenen Werte noch an den PC übertragen. Dazu setzen wir das Wort eprom2com ein:

```
: eprom2com eprom> >com 1 waitms ;
```

```
: main initCom 20 1 do I eprom2com loop ;
```

Bevor die Daten Byte für Byte über die COM-Schnittstelle übertragen werden können, muss diese initialisiert werden. Dies geschieht mit dem Wort initCom. Beim Senden der Bytes muss das Timing beachtet werden: Das Übertragen eines Bytes über die serielle Schnittstelle dauert eine gewisse Zeit.

Während des Sendevorgangs arbeitet der Mikrocontroller aber schon sein Programmweiter ab. Würde man auf den Befehl 1 waitms verzichten, würde der Mikrocontroller die nächste Übertragung starten wollen, bevor das letzte Byte vollständig übertragen wäre.

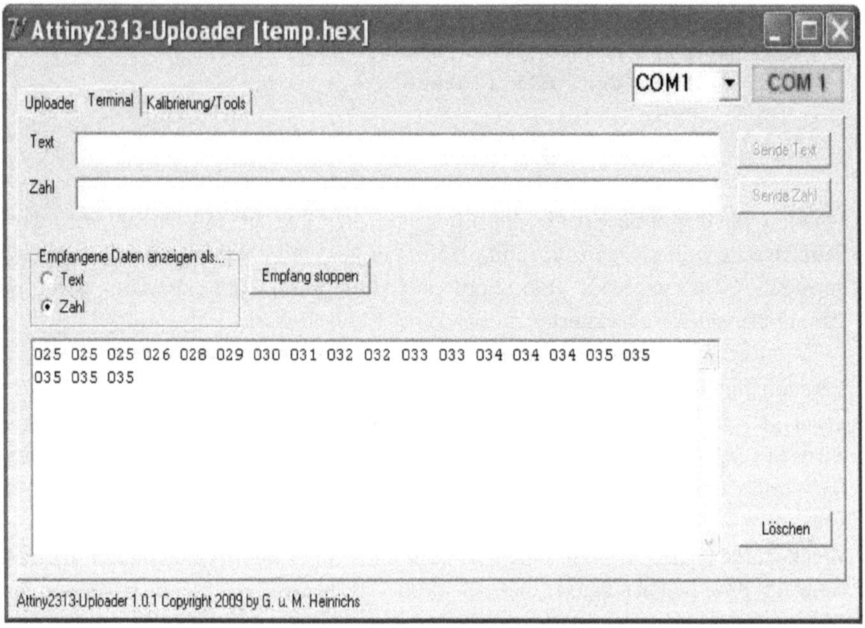

Bild 15: Das Uploader Window

Wenn wir nun das Terminalprogramm von UPLOADER laufen lassen, werden sämtliche Messwerte in weniger als 1 Sekunde an den Computer übertragen. **Bild 15** zeigt das Ergebnis einer solchen Übertragung. Deutlich erkennt man, dass die Temperaturwerte zunächst konstant bleiben und dann rasch ansteigen. Wie ist das zustande gekommen?

Während des Messvorgangs wurde eine Lampe direkt über den LM75 gehalten; dadurch wurde dieser stark erwärmt. In Abb. 3 sind die Ergebnisse mit einem Tabellenkalkulationsprogramm graphisch dargestellt worden.

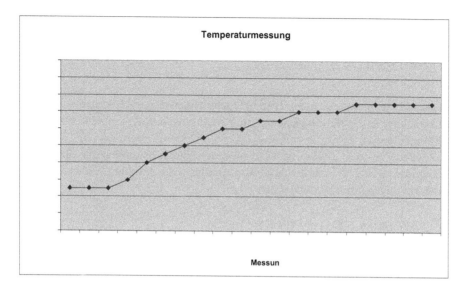

Bild 16: Sammlung von Temperaturdaten

8 MikroForth-Variablen

Zum kurzfristigen Speichern und zur Übergabe von Werten von einem Wort zum anderen ist der Stack bestens geeignet. Zum langfristigen Speichern bietet sich eher das EEPROM des Attiny an.

Allerdings ist es recht mühselig, sich die unterschiedlichen Adressen für die zu speichernden Werte zu merken. Abhilfe schaffen hier **Variable**. Sie werden in MikroForth folgendermaßen deklariert:

```
variable <Variablenname>
```

Die Variablendeklaration kann nicht innerhalb einer Doppelpunkt-definition stehen; das Schlüsselwort variable muss am Anfang einer Zeile stehen. Pro Zeile kann jeweils immer nur eine einzige Variable deklariert werden und am Ende der Zeile braucht kein Semikolon stehen.

Der Compiler vergibt für jede Variable eine Nummer zwischen 0 und 126, die als EEPROM-Adresse dient; die EEPROM-Zelle mit der Adresse 127 ist für den OSCCAL-Wert reserviert. Zudem erzeugt der Compiler für jede Variable ein Wort mit gleichem Namen. Dieses Wort hat nur eine einzige Aufgabe: Es legt die zugehörige Adresse auf den Stack.

An einem Beispiel wollen wir uns die Benutzung von Variablen anschauen:

```
variable KontoNr
: ablegen   129       KontoNr >eprom ;
: holen     KontoNr   eprom> ;
: main      ablegen   holen . ;
```

In der ersten Zeile wird die Variable KontoNr deklariert. In der zweiten Zeile wird durch das Wort KontoNr die zugehörige Adresse auf den Stack gelegt. Wenn KontoNr als erste Variable deklariert worden ist, dann ist diese Adresse $00. Durch das nachfolgende Wort >eprom wird die Zahl 129 unter der EEPROM-Adresse $00 gespeichert.

In der dritten Zeile wird die Zahl 129 wieder aus der EEPROM-Zelle $00 geholt und auf den Stack gelegt. Das Wort KontoNr kann hier wieder als Stellvertreter für die zugehörige EEPROM-Adresse angesehen werden.

Durch die Einführung von Variablen ändert sich der Quellcode im Wesentlichen nicht; er wird aber viel übersichtlicher. Man beachte: Da bei einer EEPROM-Zelle nur eine beschränkte Anzahl von Schreibvorgängen durchgeführt werden kann, sollte man das Wort holen sparsam einsetzen. Von daher sollten die MikroForth-Variablen eher als Konstanten-Speicher angesehen werden.

Im Prinzip könnten die Variablen auch zur Adressierung von SRAM- oder auch Flash-Registern benutzt werden. Davon ist aber dringend abzuraten. Der Compiler vergibt nämlich die Adressen der Reihe nach, bei 0 beginnend. So ist es fast sicher, dass unkontrolliert wichtige Statusregister oder auch Teile des Programms auf diese Weise überschrieben würden. Die Folgen wären fatal.

Aufgabe 1

Geben Sie das obige Beispiel ein und testen Sie es. Schauen Sie sich mit dem Vokabular-Editor auch das Wort **KontoNr** an.

9 Der Compiler von MikroForth

FORTH ist von der Struktur her eine einfache Sprache; deswegen ist es auch nicht schwer, die Funktionsweise unseres Forth-Compilers nachzuvollziehen.

Ausgangspunkt unserer Betrachtungen soll ein kleines FORTH-Programm sein, das wir schon im Kapitel über die Portbefehle kennen gelernt haben, die Datei **"schalten.frth"**:

```
: schalten begin Ta0? 6 swap outPortD 0 until ;

: vorbereiten 6 1 DDBitD ;

: main vorbereiten schalten ;
```

Durch dieses Programm wird eine Leuchtdiode an Port D.6 durch den Taster Ta0 ein- und ausgeschaltet.

Wir öffnen diese Datei und betätigen die Interpretieren-Schaltfläche. Dadurch werden die neuen Wörter der Doppelpunktdefinitionen in das Vokabular eingetragen.

Dies können wir leicht überprüfen, indem wir oben links auf die Lasche "Vokabular editieren" klicken.

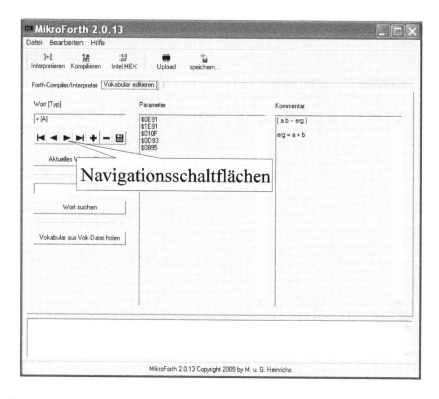

Bild 17: Das MikroForth Fenster

In diesem Editor können wir alle Wörter des Vokabulars anschauen; darüber hinausgehend können wir hier bestehende Wörter auch abändern oder sogar auch neue Wörter erzeugen, aber darauf wollen wir erst in einem späteren Kapitel zu sprechen kommen.

Betätigen wir nun die ▶| Schaltfläche, gelangen wir zum letzten Wort des Vokabulars; hier finden wir unser Wort "vorbereiten". Im Parameterfeld entdecken wir die Worte, durch die vorbereiten im Rahmen der Doppelpunkt-definition beschrieben worden ist. Beim **Interpretieren** wird also im Wesentlichen nur umstrukturiert: aus einer Textzeile werden das definierte Wort und die zugehörigen Parameter herausgeschält.

Auch das neue Wort schalten können wir uns anschauen, dazu müssen wir nur die Schaltfläche ◀ betätigen; dadurch gelangen wir zu dem vorletzten Wort des Vokabulars. Indem wir diese Schaltfläche immer wieder betätigen, können wir uns alle

Wörter des Vokabulars anschauen. Dabei fällt auf, dass es zwei Typen von Wörtern gibt:

1. **F-Wörter**: Ihre Parameter bestehen selbst wieder aus Wörtern. Sie sind aus Doppelpunktdefinitionen hervorgegangen.
2. **A-Wörter**: Ihre Parameter bestehen aus Maschinencode. Dieser Maschinencode wurde mithilfe eines Assemblers erzeugt.

Da unser Mikrocontroller nur Maschinencode verarbeiten kann, muss der gesamte FORTH-Quellcode auf solche A-Wörter zurückgeführt werden. Das ist die Aufgabe des **Compilers**. Wie er dabei vorgeht, das schauen wir uns nun anhand des obigen Beispiels etwas genauer an. Dazu klicken wir erst einmal auf die Lasche "Compiler/Interpreter" und gelangen so wieder in die gewohnte Betriebsart von MikroForth.

Ausgangspunkt unserer Betrachtungen ist zunächst das Wort main. Mit diesem Wort soll ja auch der Mikrocontroller seine Arbeit beginnen. Das Wort main ruft die Wörter vorbereiten und schalten auf.

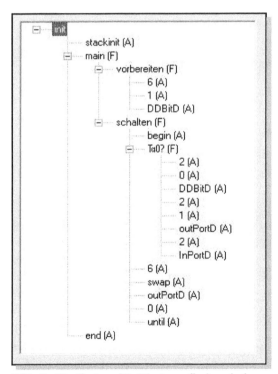

Bild 18: Wo die A und F-Worte zu finden sind

Die Parameter von **vorbereiten** sind sämtlich A-Wörter; dagegen taucht unter den Parametern von schalten noch das F-Wort Ta0? auf. Auch dieses muss wieder analysiert werden; es besteht nur aus A-Wörtern.

Derartige Analysen können in Form eines Baums verdeutlicht werden. **Bild 18** zeigt den Baum für unser Programm. Allerdings besteht die Wurzel unseres Baums nicht aus dem Wort main, sondern aus dem Wort init. Das hat folgenden Grund:

Unabhängig von den speziellen Aufgaben, welches ein FORTH-Programm zu erfüllen hat, gibt es einige Aufgaben, welche immer ausgeführt werden sollen. In unserem Fall muss vor der Ausführung von main der Stack eingerichtet werden; dies geschieht durch das Wort stackinit. Nach der Ausführung von **main** soll der Mikrocontroller stets in eine Endlosschleife übergehen; dazu dient das Wort end. Natürlich hätte man diese Aufgabe auch dem Anwender überlassen können, aber so ist es bequemer und sicherer.

Das Wort **init** ruft also zuerst **stackinit** auf, dann das Wort main und schließlich das Wort end. Bei Bedarf könnte man sogar das Wort init um weitere Standardaufgaben ergänzen, indem man das bestehende Wort init durch ein neues überschreibt.

Betätigt man nun die "Kompilieren"-Schaltfläche, wird der Baum aus **Bild 18** rekursiv nach A-Wörtern durchsucht; die zugehörigen Parameter, d. h. die entsprechenden Maschinencodes, werden in die Maschinencode-Tabelle eingetragen. Dabei wird die Startadresse dieser Maschinenprogramme zusätzlich in der **Adresszuweisungstabelle** festgehalten.

Mithilfe dieser Zuweisungstabelle kann u. a. kontrolliert werden, ob ein A-Wort schon eingetragen (kompiliert) wurde oder nicht; auf diese Weise wird vermieden, dass ein und dasselbe Wort mehrfach kompiliert wird.

Die Maschinenprogramme der A-Wörter enden alle mit dem ret-Befehl (Code $0895). Deswegen können sie als Unterprogramme aufgerufen werden. Beim Kompilieren der F-Wörter werden die als Parameter auftauchenden A-Wörter durch entsprechende Unterprogrammaufrufe ersetzt. Aus den Parametern

6

1

DDBitD

des Wortes "vorbereiten" wird z. B. der Code

rcall <Adresse von 6> rcall <Adresse von 1> rcall <Adresse von DDBitD> ret

erzeugt, natürlich in bereits assemblierter Form. Auch hier wird wieder von der Adresszuweisungstabelle Gebrauch gemacht.

Wie wir sehen, endet dieses Programmteil ebenfalls mit einem ret-Befehl; deswegen kann auch dieses Programmteil seinerseits wieder als Unterprogramm aufgerufen werden. Genau diesen Prozess führt der Compiler aus, wenn er in einem zweiten Lauf den Baumnach F-Wörtern durchsucht. Sie werden dann abhängig von Reihenfolge und Suchtiefe in die Adresszuweisungstabelle und die Maschinecodetabelle eingetragen. So wird z. B. das Wort Tao? vor dem Wort schalten eingetragen; es steht zwar hinter dem Wort schalten, liegt aber tiefer im Suchbaum.

Von der Maschinencodetabelle zum HEX-Code ist es nur ein kleiner Schritt. Er bedeutet in gewisser Weise nur eine andere Schreibweise. In der Tat muss zum Brennen dieser Schritt sogar wieder rückgängig gemacht werden.
Es ist sehr lehrreich, das Ergebnis eines solchen Kompiliervorgangs einmal detailliert anschauen. Dazu betrachten wir allerdings nicht den Maschinencode selbst, sondern den zugehörigen Assemblercode; diesen lassen wir uns aus dem HEX-Code mithilfe eines so genannten Disassemblers erzeugen. Wir legen allerdings ein etwas kürzeres Beispiel zugrunde:

FORTH-Quelltext:

```
: main 5 5 + . ;
```

HEX-Code:
```
:1000000029C01895189518951895189518954C
:100010001895189518951895189518951895189578
:100020001895189518951895A0E6B0E0089505E084
:100030000D9308950E911E91010F0D9308951FEFDA
:100040000E9117BB08BB0895FFCFF1DFF0DFF2DFA1
:0C005000F6DF0895E9DFF9DFF7DF08951F
:00000001FF
```

Assemblercode:

```
                    rjmp    avr002A
                    reti
                    reti
                    reti
                    reti
                    reti
                    reti
                    reti
                    reti
                    reti
                    reti
                    reti
                    reti
                    reti
                    reti
                    reti
                    reti
                    reti
                    reti
avr0014:            ldi     XL, 0x60
                    ldi     XH, 0x00
                    ret
avr0017:            ldi     r16, 0x05
                    st      X+, r16
                    ret
avr001A:            ld      r16, -X
                    ld      r17, -X
                    add     r16, r17
                    st      X+, r16
                    ret
avr001F:            ldi     r17, 0xFF
                    ld      r16, -X
                    out     DDRB, r17
                    out     PORTB, r16
                    ret
avr0024:            rjmp    $
avr0025:            rcall   avr0017
                    rcall   avr0017
                    rcall   avr001A
                    rcall   avr001F
                    ret
avr002A:            rcall   avr0014
                    rcall   avr0025
                    rcall   avr0024
                    ret
```

Bild 19: Der Assembler-Code

Das Programm beginnt mit dem Befehl rjmp $002A, einem Sprung zur Adresse $002A. (Die folgenden reti-Befehle übergehen wir an dieser Stelle; im Zusammenhang mit den Interrupts werden wir noch ausführlich auf ihre Bedeutung zu sprechen kommen.)

Bei der Adresse $002A beginnt das Unterprogramm zu init:

```
rcall $0014    ; stackinit
rcall $0025    ; main
rcall $0024    ; end
```

Als nächstes wird also das Unterprogramm stackinit aufgerufen; hier wird der Zeiger für den Stack initialisiert; als Zeiger wird hier das Registerpaar (XH, XL) benutzt. Der Stackzeiger X wird auf den Wert $0060 gesetzt; das ist die unterste Adresse des SRAMs.

Über den ret-Befehl springt das Programm wieder zurück zum nächsten Befehl des init Unterprogramms; hier wird das main-Unterprogramm aufgerufen, das bei der Adresse $0025 beginnt. Da es von einem FORTH-Wort abstammt, setzt es sich seinerseits aus lauter Unterprogrammaufrufen zusammen, abgeschlossen von einem ret-Befehl.

Zweimal hintereinander wird das Unterprogrammm it der Adresse $0017 aufgerufen. Hier wird jeweils die Zahl 5 auf den Stack gelegt. Dazu wird die Zahl 5 zunächst im Register r16 zwischengespeichert. Durch den Befehl st X+, r16 wird der Inhalt von r16, also unsere Zahl 5, in der Speicherzelle abgelegt, die durch X indiziert wird; anschließend wird X um 1 erhöht, weist danach also auf die nächste Speicherstelle des Stacks.

Durch die nächsten beiden Unterprogrammaufrufe von main wird die Addition ausgeführt (bei Adresse $001A) und das Ergebnis auf Port B ausgegeben (bei $001F). Dabei kann man auch erkennen, wie Zahlen vom Stack geholt werden: Durch den Befehl ld r16, X- wird z. B. der Wert aus dem von X indizierten SRAM-Register in das Register r16 geholt und der Zeigerwert um 1 vermindert; damit zeigt X nun auf den darunter liegenden Stackinhalt.

Zu guter letzt wird aus dem Unterprogramm main wieder zurückgesprungen zum Unterprogramm init. Hier geht es weiter mit rcall $0024; dort wird der Mikrocontroller in eine Endlosschleife geschickt.

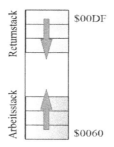

Bild 20: Der Arbeits-Stack waechst nach oben, der Return-Stack nach unten

Wer sich eingehender mit Assembler-Unterprogrammen beschäftigt hat, der weiß, dass hier ein weiterer Stack benutzt wird, der so genannte **Returnstack**. Der Stack, welchen wir bei der FORTH-Programmierung bislang betrachtet haben, wird zur Unterscheidung oft auch als **Arbeitsstack** bezeichnet. Returnstack- und Arbeitsstack sind beide im SRAM angesiedelt; sie teilen ihn sich:

Während der Arbeitsstack bei $0060 beginnt und dann die darüber liegenden Zellen belegt, fängt der Returnstack bei $00DF an und belegt dann die darunter liegenden Zellen (**Bild 20**). Auf diese Weise wird die Gefahr einer Kollision der beiden Stacks möglichst klein gehalten. Im Gegensatz zum Arbeitsstack muss man sich um die Verwaltung des Stackpointers Z beim Returnstack nicht kümmern; dies übernehmen die Befehle rcall und ret selbstständig.

Wesentliche Idee unseres Forth-Compilers ist also die Verschachtelung von Unterprogrammen. F-Wörter bestehen nur aus Unterprogramm-Aufrufen; diese können auf F- oder auch auf A-Wörter verweisen. Letztlich müssen diese Unterprogrammaufrufe natürlich immer bei A-Wörtern auskommen; denn nur hier findet sich der Maschinencode, der nicht auf ein anderes Wort verweist, sondern tatsächlich "Arbeit verrichtet".

Dieses einfache Konzept führt natürlich zu Einschränkungen. Manche Kontroll-strukturen (IF ELSE-THEN (Kein Versehen bei der Reihenfolge!) oder BEGIN-WHILE-REPEAT lassen sich damit auch nicht realisieren. Dafür bietet dieses Konzept aber die Möglichkeit, recht unkompliziert neue A-Wörter in das Vokabular einzufügen.
Wenn Sie daran interessiert sind, sollten Sie gleich das übernächste Kapitel lesen. Im folgenden Kapitel wollen wir uns nämlich etwas eingehender damit beschäftigen, wie überhaupt Kontrollstrukturen realisiert werden können.

10 Funktionsweise der Do-Loop-Schleife

Wir gehen aus von folgendem Beispiel:

```
10 3 do Bef1 Bef2 loop Bef3
```

Dem entsprechen im Speicher die Unterprogrammaufrufe

```
rcall <10> rcall <3> rcall <do> rcall <Bef1> rcall <Bef2> rcall
<loop> rcall <Bef3>.
```

Dabei bedeuten die spitzen Klammern "Adresse von...".

Durch die ersten beiden Unterprogramme werden der Startwert (3) und der Endwert (10) des Schleifenindex auf den Arbeitsstack gelegt. Jedesmal, wenn ein Unterprogramm aufgerufen wird, merkt sich der Mikrocontroller die Adresse des nächsten Befehls, indem er sie auf den Returnstack legt. Wenn also das do-Unterprogramm aufgerufen wird, wird die Adresse von rcall <Bef1> auf den Returnstack gelegt.

Genauer betrachtet besteht diese Adresse aus zwei Bytes; wir bezeichnen diese Adressen als *AdrBef1(high)* und *AdrBef1(low)*. Unmittelbar nach dem Aufruf des do-Unterprogramms sehen unsere beiden Stacks also so aus:

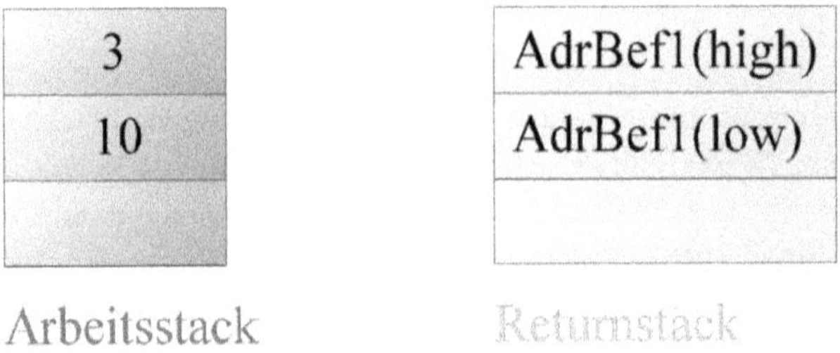

Arbeitsstack Returnstack

Bild 21: Daten auf dem Arbeitsstack, Adressen auf dem Returnstack

Alles, was das do-Unterprogramm leisten muss, ist dafür zu sorgen, dass der Mikrocontroller sich dieses Adresspaar langfristig merkt; nur so kann gewährleistet werden, dass er am Ende eines Schleifendurchlaufs wieder zum Anfang der Schleife kehren kann. Dieses Merken kann nicht über Arbeitsregister wie z. B. r16 geschehen; denn diese könnten z. B. durch das Unterprogramm von Bef1 oder Bef2 überschrieben werden.

Ein sicherer Ort zum langfristigen Merken ist der Returnstack. Hier liegt unser Adresspaar zwar schon, aber am Ende des do-Unterprogramms wird dieses Adresspaar durch den ret-Befehl vom Returnstack in den Programmzähler geschoben und verschwindet dabei vom Returnstack.
Damit ist aber auch schon die Lösung in Sicht: Das Adresspaar auf dem Returnstack muss von do verdoppelt werden; so steht die Kopie auch nach der Ausführung von do noch zur Verfügung. Ebenso müssen auch die beiden Schleifenindizes gesichert werden. Dies leistet der folgende Assemblercode:

```
.def AdrH = r16
.def AdrL = r17
.def A = r18
.def E = r19


ld A,-x              ; Startindex vom Parameterstack
ld E,-x              ; Schleifenende vom Parameterstack
pop AdrH pop AdrL
                     ; Returnadresse vom Returnstack
push AdrL push AdrH
                     ; und wieder drauf (für LOOP)
push E push A
                     ; Schleifenparameter auf Returnstack
push AdrL push AdrH
                     ; Returnadresse noch einmal auf den Stack
ret
                     ; zum nächsten Befehl
```

Unmittelbar vor dem ret-Befehl des do-Unterprogramms und unmittelbar danach sieht der Returnstack dann so aus:

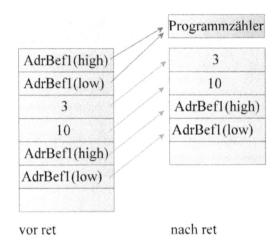

| AdrBefl(high) |
| AdrBefl(low) |
| 3 |
| 10 |
| AdrBefl(high) |
| AdrBefl(low) |
| |

| Programmzähler |
| 3 |
| 10 |
| AdrBefl(high) |
| AdrBefl(low) |
| |

vor ret   nach ret

Bild 22: Return-Stack vor und nach einem Interrupt

Durch den nun folgenden Unterprogrammaufruf rcall <Bef1> wird nun das Adresspaar von rcall <Bef2> auf den Returnstack gelegt; beim Rücksprung verschwindet es aber wieder. Und so geht es weiter, bis das folgende loop-Unterprogramm aufgerufen wird.

```
.def AdrH = r16
.def AdrL = r17          ; Returnstack
.def A = r18             ; Schleife: aktueller Index
.def E = r19             ; Endwert des Schleifenindex
.def nextAdrH = r20      ; Adresse von Bef3
.def nextAdrL = r21
    pop nextAdrH                    ; Adresse von Bef3 retten
pop nextAdrL
pop A                              ; aktueller Index vom
                                   ; Returnstack holen
pop E                              ; Endwert vom Returnstack
pop ZH                   ; Adresse von Bef1
pop ZL                   ; vom Returnstack
cp A, E
breq loopende            ; wenn A=E dann nach
                                   ; loopende springen
                                   ; sonst (A < E)
push ZL                  ; und wieder drauf
push ZH                  ; (für nächstes LOOP)
```

```
inc A
push E push A              ; Schleifenparameter
                           ; auf Returnstack
    ijmp loopende:         ; Sprung nach Adresse,
    push nextAdrL          ; die in Z steht (s. o.)
    push nextAdrH          ; keine zusätzliche Adr
                           ; auf Stapel!
ret                        ; zum nächsten Befehl
```

In dieser Situation liegt das Adresspaar von rcall <Bef3> auf dem Returnstack. Das wird zunächst einmal vom Returnstack geholt und in Arbeitsregistern (nextAdrH und nextAdrL) zwischengespeichert; die Schleifenindizes 3 und 10 werden ebenso in Arbeitsregistern zwischengelagert (A bzw. E) .

Die Werte *AdrBef1(high)* und *AdrBef1(low)* werden in das Registerpaar Z geschoben; dies wird einen indirekten Sprung zumBefehl rcall <Bef1> ermöglichen. Nun wird kontrolliert, ob der aktuelle Schleifenindex (3) kleiner als der Endwert (10) ist. Da dies der Fall ist, wird der Schleifenindex (3) um 1 erhöht, das Adresspaar und die Indizes für einen möglichen weiteren Schleifendurchlauf wieder auf den Returnstack gelegt und der indirekte Sprung ijmp ausgeführt. Der bedeutet einen Sprung an die Adresse, welche im Registerpaar Z steht, also zu rcall <Bef1>.

Dies wiederholt sich solange, bis der aktuelle Indexwert gleich dem Endwert (10) ist. In diesem Fall wird das zwischengespeicherte Adresspaar von rcall <Bef3> wieder auf den Returnstack gelegt; so springt das Programm durch den letzten Befehl von loop, nämlich dem ret-Befehl, wie gewünscht nicht mehr an den Anfang der Schleife, sondern zum Unterprogrammaufruf von Bef3.

Aufgabe

Das Wort do kann auch als F-Wort geschrieben werden:

```
: do swap R> R> over over >R
    >R rot >R rot >R >R >R ;
```

Schlagen Sie die Bedeutung von R> und >R im Vokabular nach und machen Sie sich die Funktionsweise dieser Befehlsfolge anhand von Stackdiagrammen klar.

11 Herstellen von A-Wörtern

Bisher haben wir uns nur darum gekümmert, wie man F-Wörter erzeugt. Dies geschah über die Doppelpunktdefinition im Rahmen des üblichen Interpretier- und Kompiliervorgangs. Für viele Anwendungen ist das auch ausreichend.

Es kann aber vorkommen, dass die im Vokabular zur Verfügung gestellten Wörter nicht ausreichen. In diesem Fall ist es zweckmäßig, das Problem genau zu lokalisieren und dafür ein passendes A-Wort selbst zu erzeugen. Wir wollen dies an einem einfachen Beispiel verdeutlichen.

Die Aufgabe möge darin bestehen, ein Wort zu erzeugen, welches sämtliche Werte auf dem Stack über die serielle Schnittstelle ausgibt; ein solches Wort könnte gut zu Testzwecken eingesetzt werden. Schleifenstrukturen und Wörter für die COM-Ausgabe und das Arbeiten mit dem SRAM stehen im Vokabular schon zur Verfügung. Was noch fehlt, ist ein Wort, dass die Anzahl der Werte auf dem Stack angibt; diese Anzahl bezeichnet man manchmal auch als **Stacktiefe**.

Zur Ermittlung dieser Stacktiefe soll nun ein neues Wort stackcount erzeugt werden. Hierzu muss auf den Stackpointer X zurückgegriffen werden; da der bislang durch kein Forth-Wort erfasst ist, muss stackcount mit Maschinencode erzeugt werden. Wir müssen also ein A-Wort herstellen.

Der nötige Assemblercode sieht so aus:

```
.def stackcount = r16    ; r0 bis r15 reserviert
                         ; für Interrupts
mov stackcount, XL       ; Stackpointer XL
                         ; nach stackcount
subi stackcount, $60     ; Stack-Startadresse
                         ; $60 subtrahieren
st x+, stackcount        ; Ergebnis auf Stack
                         ; legen
ret
```

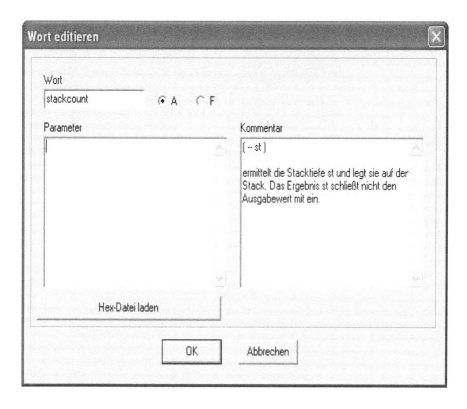

Bild 23: Ein Wort editieren

Wir assemblieren den Code, zum Beispiel mit Studio 4, und speichern die Hex-Datei unter dem Namen "stackcount.hex" ab. Nun öffnen wir unser Programm MikroForth und klicken auf die Lasche "Vokabular editieren".

Auf der Navigationsleiste klicken wir die +-Schaltfläche an; es öffnet sich ein Fenster zum Editieren von Wörtern; dort tragen wir den Namen des Wortes und den Kommentar so ein wie in Abb. 1 zu sehen.

Nun laden wir den vorbereiteten Hex-Code in das Parameterfeld: Dazu betätigen wir die Schaltfläche "Hex-Datei laden" unterhalb des Parameterfeldes und öffnen unsere Datei "stackcount.hex". Das Editier-Fenster sieht dann so aus:

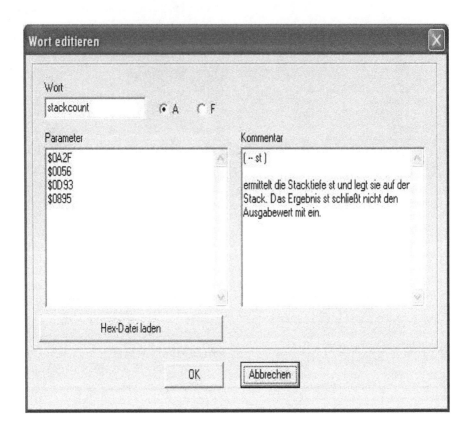

Bild 24: Mit Parametern

Jetzt bestätigen wir noch die Eingabe mit der OK-Schaltfläche. Damit ist unser neues A-Wort fertig. Es befindet sich allerdings nur im temporären Vokabular. Um es dauerhaft zu speichern, klicken wir abschließend auf die Disketten-Schaltfläche in der Navigationsleiste.

Mithilfe von stackcount können wir jetzt leicht das Wort stack2com schreiben, welches den Stack über die COM-Schnittstelle ausgibt:

```
: stack2com initcom stackcount
          1 do I 95 + sram> >com 250
               waitms loop ;
```

Was geschieht hier? Zunächst wird die COM-Schnittstelle initialisiert; anschließend wird die Stacktiefe ermittelt und auf den Stack gelegt. Zusammen mit der folgenden

Zahl 1 bildet sie End- und Startwert der folgenden do-loop-Schleife. Innerhalb der Schleife wird zum Schleifenindex jeweils die Zahl 95 addiert; das Ergebnis ist die Adresse des jeweiligen Stackregisters im SRAM.

Der Inhalt dieses Registers wird dann mit dem Befehl sram> auf den Stack gelegt und von >com an die serielle Schnittstelle weitergereicht. Eine kurze Wartezeit - wenn auch nicht so lange, wie hier angegeben - ist erforderlich, damit die COM-Übertragung eines Bytes nicht durch die Übertragung des nächsten gestört wird.

Zum Austesten benutzen wir das folgende main-Wort:

```
: main 11 22 33 44 55 66 77 88 99 stack2com ;
```

Hierdurch werden die Zahlen 11, 22 bis 99 auf den Stack gelegt und gleich darauf durch stack2com ausgegeben. Das können wir leicht nachkontrollieren, indem wir im Uploader-Programm das Terminal-Programm aktivieren.

Attiny2313-Uploader [temp.hex]		
Uploader Terminal | Kalibrierung |	COM1 ▾	COM 1
Text [ ]		Sende Text
Zahl [ ]		Sende Zahl
Empfangene Daten anzeigen als... ○ Text ● Zahl	[Empfang stoppen]	
011 022 033 044 055 066 077 088 099		
		Löschen
Attiny2313-Uploader 0.4c Copyright 2009 by G. u. M. Heinrichs		

Bild 25: Daten im Uploader-Fenster

12 Rekursion mit MikroForth

Das einfache Konzept unseres FORTH-Compilers bedingt, dass ein Forth-Wort sich nicht direkt selbst aufrufen kann. Lassen wir z. B. das folgende Programm

```
: rektest 1 . rektest ;
: main rektest ;
```

interpretieren, so erhält man die Meldung:

Fehler: Das Wort "rektest" wurde im Vokabular
nicht gefunden.
"rektest" wurde nicht im Vokabular eingetragen!
Warnung: Interpretiervorgang abgebrochen...

Allerdings können wir die Kenntnisse über die Art und Weise, wie MikroForth arbeitet, ausnutzen, um mit einem Trick doch noch eine Rekursion zu realisieren. Dazu rufen wir aus der Doppelpunktdefinition von rektest nicht das Wort rektest selbst auf, sondern ein anderes Wort zu_rektest, welches seinerseits dafür sorgt, dass rektest ausgeführt wird. Allerdings kann das Wort zu_rektest das Wort rektest nicht wie üblich aufrufen; dies hätte nur eine Fehlermeldung wie oben zur Folge.

Wie kann dieser Aufruf von rektest nun anders realisiert werden? Hierzu nutzen wir aus, dass die Adresse des Wortes, das als nächstes auszuführen ist, auf dem Returnstack zu liegen hat. Das Wort zu_rektest muss also nichts anderes leisten, als die Adresse von rektest auf den Returnstack zu legen.

An einem konkreten Beispiel soll die Vorgehensweise erläutert werden. Die Zahlen von 1 bis 32 sollen ausgegeben werden, zuerst vorwärts zählend und dann rückwärts.

```
: zu_rektest 0 122 >r >r ;
: rektest dup dup . 255 waitms 1 + dup
          32 equal skipIf
          zu_rektest . 255 waitms ;
: main 1 rektest . ;
```

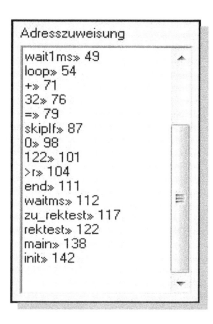

Bild 26: Adress-Zuweisungen

Das Wort zu_rektest legt die Adresse von rektest auf den Returnstack. Diese Adresse besteht hier aus dem Highbyte 0 und dem Lowbyte 122. Wie gelangt man an diese Adresse? Dazu braucht man nach dem Kompilieren nur die Adresszuweisungstabelle anschauen.

Die drittletzte Zeile in **Bild 26** zeigt, dass die gesuchte Adresse 122 ist. Für die Adressfindung ist es nicht gleichgültig, welche Werte für die beiden Adressbytes in der Definition von zu_rektest zunächst eingesetzt worden sind. Eine nachträgliche Kontrolle mit der gefundenen Adresse empfiehlt sich also.
Die Rekursionstiefe wird durch die Größe des SRAMs begrenzt.

13 Interrupts

MikroForth unterstützt auch das Interrupt-Konzept des Attiny-Mikrocontrollers. Allerdings gibt es im Standardvokabular nur Wörter für die Interrupts INT0, INT1 und T0OVF (Timer/Couter0 Overflow). Einer Erweiterung des Vokabulars für andere Interrupts steht jedoch nichts im Weg.

Am Beispiel des INT0-Interrupts soll nun dargelegt werden, wie die Interrupt-Programmierung in MikroForth erfolgt. Für grundlegende Fragen zum Interrupt-Konzept wird auf das entsprechende Kapitel verwiesen.

Und das soll unser Programm leisten: Ein an Port D.6 angeschlossener Beeper soll die ganze Zeit über tönen. Eine LED an Port B.0 soll währenddessen über eine fallende Flanke an Ta0 geschaltet werden; ob durch diesen Tastendruck diese LED ein- oder ausgeschaltet wird, soll durch den Zustand von Ta1 festgelegt werden.
Wie üblich muss der INT0-Interrupt zunächst initialisiert werden. Dies geschieht durch das Wort initInt0:

```
initInt0            ( f - )
```

Der Wert von f entscheidet darüber, ob der Interrupt durch eine fallende (f = 0) oder steigende Flanke (f = 1) am INT0-Eingang (Port D.2) erfolgt. Durch die Initialisierung mit initInt0 werden auch folgende Aktionen erledigt:

- **Port D.2 als Eingang konfigurieren,**
- **Port D.2 auf high legen,**
- **Interrupts freigeben.**

In unserem Fall muss f = 0 sein, denn durch das Drücken von Ta0 geht D.2 von high nach low über.
Wird der INT0-Interrupt ausgelöst, wird nun automatisch das Wort int0 ausgeführt. Die Bezeichnung dieses Wortes ist fest vorgegeben. Der Wortkörper kann jedoch beliebig vom Benutzer programmiert werden; jedoch muss dabei folgende Form eingehalten werden:

```
: int0 pushreg <benutzerdefinierter Teil>
       popreg reti ;
```

Das hat folgenden Grund: Der Interrupt wird in der Regel mitten in der Ausführung eines anderen Wortes erfolgen. Damit die Registerinhalte r16-r29, welche dieses andere Wort womöglich benutzt, nicht verloren gehen, werden sie als erstes durch das Wort pushreg gerettet. Dazu kopiert pushreg deren Inhalte in die Register r2 bis r15, die bei den A-Wörtern nicht zum Einsatz kommen (dürfen).

In dem benutzerdefinierten Bereich von int0 können jetzt alle Wörter beliebig benutzt werden. Am Ende werden durch popreg alle Register r16 bis r29 wieder hergestellt; so kann das in seiner Ausführung unterbrochene Wort korrekt weiterarbeiten.
Beim Auslösen des Interrupts wird der Attiny für weitere Interrupts global gesperrt. Um ihn wieder frei zu geben für erneute Interrupts, muss die Definition von int0 mit dem Wort reti enden.

In unserem Fall sieht die Definition des Wortes int0 so aus:

```
: int0 pushreg Ta1? . popreg reti ;
```

Der benutzerdefinierte Teil ist sehr kurz: Durch Ta1? wird der Zustand des Tasters Ta1 abgefragt. Ist Ta1 gedrückt, wird eine 0 auf den Stapel gelegt und diese dann an Port B ausgegeben; andernfalls wird eine 1 auf den Stapel gelegt und dann ausgegeben. Die LED wird also, je nachdem ob Ta1 gedrückt ist oder nicht, ein- bzw. ausgeschaltet.
Das gesamte Programm sieht dann so aus:

```
: int0 pushreg Ta1? . popreg reti ;
: BeeperAnAus 6 1 outportD 10 waitms
              6 0 outPortD 10 waitms ;
: main 6 1 DDBitD 0 initInt0
       begin BeeperAnAus 0 until ;
```

Im Hauptprogramm wird durch eine Endlosschleife für eine Schwingung mit der Periodendauer 2 ⊠ 10 ms am Port D.6 gesorgt.

Aufgabe
Testen Sie das Programm aus; betätigen Sie dazu den Taster Ta0 mehrfach bei unterschiedlichen Tasterzuständen von Ta1. Lassen Sie nun den reti-Befehl weg und führen Sie den Test erneut durch.

14 MikroForth einstellen

MikroForth erlaubt folgende Anpassungen:

1. Programm zum Uploaden
2. Warnhinweis bei Überschreiben von Wörtern
3. Auswahl des Separators in der Adressenzuweisungstabelle
4. Anzeigen der Adressen im HEX- oder Dezimalformat

Die entsprechenden Einstellungen sind in der Datei forth2.ini gespeichert. Sie können dort bei Bedarf mit einem Editor geändert werden.

Programm zum Uploaden
Soll auf das Programm "Uploader.exe" zurückgegriffen werden, besteht der Eintrag in der ini-Datei einfach aus einem Minuszeichen:

    externuploader=-

Ansonsten wird hinter das Gleichheitszeichen der Name des gewünschten Programms mitsamt dem vollständigen Pfad angegeben.

Warnhinweis bei Überschreiben von Wörtern
Häufig müssen einzelne Wörter des aktuellen Vokabulars überschrieben werden. Ist der Eintrag

    ueberschreiben=1

dann gibt MikroForth einen entsprechender Warnhinweis in einem Meldungsfenster. Sie haben dann die Möglichkeit, das Überschreiben zu unterbinden. Wenn Sie den Wert 0 hinter das Gleichheitszeichen schreiben, dann erfolgt nur ein Hinweis im Statusbereich und das alte Wort wird überschrieben.
Sie können diesen Parameter auch über Bearbeiten - Einstellungen ändern.

Auswahl des Separators in der Adressenzuweisungstabelle

In der Adresszuweisungstabelle befindet sich zwischen dem Forth-Wort und der zugehörigen Adresse ein so genannter **Separator**. Standardmäßig ist dies ein Doppel-Größer-Zeichen mit dem ASCII-Code 187. Sie können dieses Zeichen in der Zeile

   separator=187

ändern. Geben Sie dazu hinter dem Gleichheitszeichen einen anderen Code ein. Dieser Code darf aber nicht zu einem Zeichen gehören, das im Namen eines Forth-Wortes auftaucht. Daher empfiehlt es sich, nur ASCII-Codes oberhalb von 127 zu benutzen.

Anzeigen der Adressen im HEX- oder Dezimalformat
Sie können auswählen, ob die Adressen im Hex- oder im Dezimalformat angezeigt werden sollen. Dazu wird die Zeile

   hexadressen=1

benutzt. Bei dem Eintrag 1 werden die Adressen im HEX-Format angezeigt, bei dem Eintrag 0 in dezimaler Schreibweise.
Sie können diesen Parameter auch über Bearbeiten - Einstellungen ändern

15 Forth-Vokabular

Stand: 01.11.2012

A: Assembler-Wort   **F:** Forth-Wort   **C:** Compiler-Wort

Wort	Typ	Kommentar	Stack
.	A	gibt TOS auf Port B aus; (Datenrichtungsbits von Port B werden alle auf 1gesetzt.)	(n –)
–	A	erg = a – b	(a b – erg)
/	A	dividiert a (ganzzahlig) durch b erg = a/b (ohne Rest)	(a b – erg rest)
:	C	leitet Doppelpunktdefinition ein.	
;	C	schließt Doppelpunktdefinition ab.	
<	A	a b < legt 1 (TRUE) auf den Stack, wenn a < b ist, sonst 0.	(a b – flag)
>	F	a b > legt 1 (TRUE) auf den Stack, wenn a > b ist, sonst 0.	(a b – flag)
>com	A	sendet TOS an die COM-Schnittstelle. Vorher muss die COM-Schnittstelle mit INITCOM initialisiert worden sein.	(n –)

>eprom	A	schreibt den Wert w in die Adresse a des EEPROMs. Vgl. eprom>	(w a –)
>R	A	schiebt den TOS auf den Returnstack Vgl. R>	(a –)
>sram	A	speichert den Wert w in der SRAM-Zelle mit der Adresse a	(w a –)
1 bis 255	AC	legt die Zahl auf den Stack.	(– n)
and	A	erg = a and b	(a b – erg)

Wort	Typ	Kommentar	Stack
begin ... until	A	begin Bef1 Bef2 ... Befn until wiederholt die Befehle Bef1, Bef2, ..., Befn, bis until auf TOS = 1 stößt. begin until	(–) (n –)
blink	F	*bitmuster hp* blink gibt *bitmuster* auf Port B aus, wartet *hp* Millisekunden, gibt 0 auf Port B aus und wartet wieder *hp* Millisekunden.	(b hp –)
com>	A	legt über COM-Schnittstelle empfangenes Byte auf Stack. Vgl. >com.	(– n)
DDBitB	A	*bit flag* DDBitB setzt den Anschluss bit des Ports B als	(bit flag –)

		Ausgang, wenn *flag* = 1, sonst als Eingang.	
DDBitD	A*	*bit flag* DDBitB setzt den Anschluss *bit* des Ports B als Ausgang, wenn *flag* = 1, sonst als Eingang.	(bit flag –)
DDRB	A	schreibt b in das Datenrichtungsregister des Ports B.	(b –)
DDRD	A*	schreibt d in das Datenrichtungsregister des Ports D.	(d –)
do ... loop	A	*e a* do Bef1 Bef2 ... Befn loop wiederholt die Befehle Bef1, Bef2, ..., Befn; die Schleife beginnt mit dem Index *a* und läuft bis *e* (einschließlich). Die Schleife wird mindestens einmal durchlaufen. Innerhalb der Schleife kann durch das Wort I auf den Index zurückgegriffen werden. do loop	(e a –) (–)
drop	A	entfernt den TOS	(n –)
dup	A	dupliziert den TOS	(n – n n)

Wort	Typ	Kommentar	Stack
end	A	führt eine Endlosleerschleife aus; wird für das Ende eines Programms empfohlen.	(–)

eprom>	A	liest den Wert w aus der EEPROMAdresse a und legt ihn auf den Stack Vgl. >eprom	(a – w)
getOSCCAL	A	legt den OSCCAL-Wert auf den Stack. Vgl. SetOSCCAL	(– n)
I	A	legt den Schleifenindex einer do-loopSchleife auf den Stack. Darf nur zwischen do und loop auftauchen.	(– n)
i2cread	A	Ein Wert wird vom Slave gelesen; wenn ACK = 0 ist, wird ein AcknowledgeSignal gegeben.	(ACK – Wert)
i2cstart	A	Startsignal für I2C-Bus wird gesendet (SDA von 1 auf 0; dann SCL von 1 auf 0)	(–)
i2cstop	A	initialisiert den I2C-Bus (SCL und SDA auf 1); Datenrichtungsbits für SDA (PortB.5) und SCL (PortB.7) werden gesetzt.	(–)
i2cwrite	A	Ein einzelnes Byte wird an den Slave gesendet; das Acknowledge-Signal wird auf den Stack gelegt.	(Wert/Adr – ACK)
init	F	Systemwort, darf nicht geändert oder entfernt werden.	

		initialisiert die COM-Schnittstelle:	(–)
initCom	A	D0 = RxD D1 = TxD Baudate = 9600 8 Bit kein Paritätsbit	

Wort	Typ	Kommentar	Stack
initInt0	A	*signaltyp* initInt0 konfiguriert INT0 (Port D2) als Interrupteingang und legt diesen auf High. Je nach *signaltyp*-Wert lösen unterschiedliche Eingangssignale den Interrupt aus: 0: fallende Flanke 1: steigende Flanke Interrupts werden generell zugelassen.	(signaltyp –)
initInt1	A	wie initInt0, jedoch für den Eingang INT1 (Port D3).	(signaltyp –)
initT0ovf	A	*typ preset* initT0ovf initialisiert den Timer0-Interrupt: *typ* 0: Timer stoppen/deaktivieren 1: Systemtakt/1 2: Systemtakt/8 3: Systemtakt/64 4: Systemtakt/256 5: Systemtakt/1024 6: ext. Takt, fallend an T0 7: ext. Takt, steigend an T0	(typ preset –)

		Timer-Interrupt werden freigegeben alle Interrupts werden freigegeben *preset*-Wert muss in Interruptroutine immer wieder neu gesetzt werden.	
inPortB	A	*bit* InPortB liest den Eingang *bit* des Ports B und legt 1/0 auf den Stack, wenn er High/Low ist. Vgl. DDRB und DDBitB	(bit – flag)
inPortD	A	*bit* InPortD liest den Eingang *bit* des Ports D und legt 1/0 auf den Stack, wenn er High/Low ist. Vgl. DDRD und DDBitD	(bit – flag)

Wort	Typ	Kommentar	Stack
int0	F	Dieses Wort wird aufgerufen wenn das INT0-Interrupt ausgelöst wird. Aufbau eines Interruptwortes: : int0 pushreg ... <beliebige Wörter> ... popreg reti; Während das Wort int0 ausgeführt wird, sind sämtliche Interrupts gesperrt.	(–)
int1	F	Dieses Wort wird aufgerufen, wenn das INT1-Interrupt ausgelöst wird. Kann beliebig definiert werden.	(–)

not	F	ersetzt *flag* durch sein logisches Komplement.	(*flag* –)
or	A	erg = a or b	(a b – erg)
outPortB	A	*bit flag* outPortB setzt den Ausgang *bit* des Ports B auf High/Low, wenn *flag* = 1/0 ist. Vgl. DDRB und DDBitB	(bit flag –)
outPortD	A	*bit flag* outPortD setzt den Ausgang *bit* des Ports D auf High/Low, wenn *flag* = 1/0 ist. Vgl. DDRD und DDBitD	(bit flag –)
over	A	kopiert das zweite Element des Stacks auf den TOS.	(a b – a b a)
popreg	A	Sämtliche internen Register r16-r29 werden wiederhergestellt.	(–)
pushreg	A	Sämtliche internen Register r16-r29 werden gesichert (in r2-r15).	(–)
R>	A	holt das oberste Element des Returnstacks und legt es auf den (Arbeits-) Stack. Vgl. >R	(– a)
reti	A	Interrupts werden freigegeben.	(–)
rot	A	rotiert die obersten drei Zahlen des Stacks.	(a b c – b c a)
sei	A	wie reti	
setOSCCAL	A	schreibt den Wert n in das OSCCALRegister.	(n –)

Wort	Typ	Kommentar	Stack
setTimer0	A	setzt den Preset-Wert (TCNT0) von Timer0.	(preset –)
skipIf	A	überspringt den nächsten Befehl, wenn TOS gleich 1 (TRUE) ist.	(n –)
sram>	A	legt den Wert der SRAM-Zelle a auf den Stack	(a – w)
stackInit	A	Systemwort, darf nicht geändert oder entfernt werden	
swap	A	vertauscht die beiden obersten Zahlen des Stacks.	(n m – m n)
T0ovf	F	Dieses Wort wird aufgerufen, wenn das Timer0-Overflow-Interrupt ausgelöst wird. Zum Aufbau eines Interrupt-Wortes vgl. int0. Innerhalb von T0ovf muss ggf. der Preset-Wert des Timers mit setTimer0 gesetzt werden.	(–)
Ta0?	F	Legt 1/0 auf Stack, wenn Taster Ta0 offen/geschlossen (D2=1/0) PortD.2 wird automatisch konfiguriert.	(– bit)
Ta1?	F	Legt 1/0 auf Stack, wenn Taster Ta1 offen/geschlossen (D3=1/0) PortD.3 wird automatisch konfiguriert.	
toggleB	A	toggelt das Register von Port B.	(–)

VARIABLE	C	leitet Variablendeklaration ein. Durch VARIABLE *abc* wird die Variable *abc* deklariert. Dadurch wird durch den Compiler im EEPROM ein Speicherplatz reserviert. Anschließend wird durch *abc* die Adresse von der zugehörigen Speicherstelle auf den Stapel gelegt.	
wait	F	wartet s Sekunden.	(s –)
wait1ms	A	wartet 1 Millisekunde.	(–)
waitms	F	wartet n Millisekunden.	(n –)

Wort	Typ	Kommentar	Stack
wdogOff	A	schaltet den Watchdog aus.	(–)
wdogOn	A	schaltet den Watchdog an.	(–)
xor	A	erg = a xor b	(a b – erg)
▣	A	*a b =* legt 1 (TRUE) auf den Stack, wenn *a* = *b* ist, sonst 0 (FALSE).	(a b – flag)
+	A	erg = a + b	(a b – erg)
*	F	erg = a * b	(a b – erg)

Some additional words:

This concludes the two main parts of the project.

The next pages are additional information taken from the webpage – either translated or not translated yet,

or drawings and ideas that I want to try out myself,

and still have to get the components for.

The decision had to be taken, if I delay the publication or rather see this eBook/Book as a first step, where the main parts are available,

and feedback plus additional work will improve further versions.

And here now the print book is published as well. Quicker than planned.

I hope you enjoy the eBook and and this print book,

Or even get tempted to try it out.

As said before, please
Tell amazon what you like about this project
and send a quick email to epldfpga@aol.com to mention improvements.
Thanks in advance.

Juergen Pintaske, Exeter October 2018

Appendix:

	A	B	C	D	E		F	G	H	I	K	
1	O	O	O	O	O		O	O	O	O	O	1
2	O	O	O	O	O		O	O	O	O	O	2
					RS_01	20_Vcc						
3	O	O	O	O	▢		▢	O	O	O	O	3
					RX_02	19_B7						
4	O	O	O	O	▢		▢	O	O	O	O	4
					TX_03	18_B6						
5	O	O	O	O	▢		▢	O	O	O	O	5
					A1_04	17_B5						
6	O	O	O	O	▢		▢	O	O	O	O	6
					A0_05	16_B4						
7	O	O	O	O	▢		▢	O	O	O	O	7
					D2_06	15_B3						
8	O	O	O	O	▢		▢	O	O	O	O	8
					D3_07	14_B2						
9	O	O	O	O	▢		▢	O	O	O	O	9
					D4_08	13_B1						
10	O	O	O	O	▢		▢	O	O	O	O	10
					D5_09	12_B0						
11	O	O	O	O	▢		▢	O	O	O	O	11
					GD_10	11_D6						
12	O	O	O	O	▢		▢	O	O	O	O	12
13	O	O	O	O	O		O	O	O	O	O	13
14	O	O	O	O	O		O	O	O	O	O	14
15	O	O	O	O	O		O	O	O	O	O	15
16	O	O	O	O	O		O	O	O	O	O	16
17	O	O	O	O	O		O	O	O	O	O	17
	A	B	C	D	E		F	G	H	I	K	

Appendix A: Using a small Breadboard for own project layouts

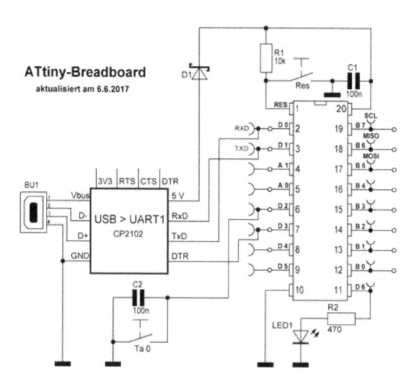

Appendix B: Minimum Circuit diagram

Appendix C: Where to get a board:
If you are interested in the purchase of one or more boards (as a kit or ready-made and tested, from about 20 Euro),
please contact Mr. Eube directly (eeube@ish.de)

Wenn Sie Interesse am Erwerb einer oder mehrerer Platinen haben (als Bausatz oder fix und fertig, ab ca. 20 Euro), wenden Sie sich bitte direkt an Herrn Eube (eeube@ish.de)

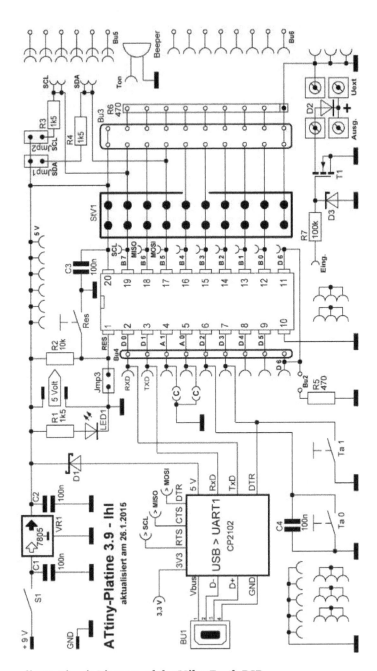

Appendix D: Circuit Diagram of the MikroForth PCB

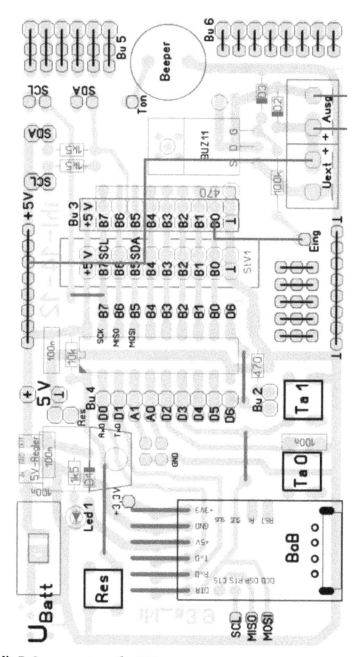

Appendix E: Components on the PCB

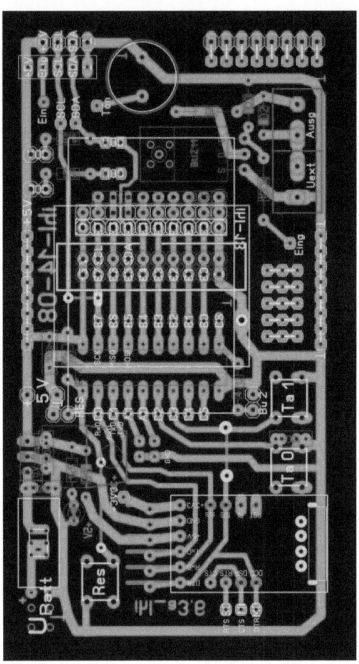

Appendix F: The PCB offered

Appendix G:

Attiny-Platine ohne Platine?!

Eine Attiny-Platine ohne Platine? Wie soll das gehen? Ganz einfach: Dank der für wenige Euro erhältlichen USB-UART-Wandler sind nur wenige Bauteile erforderlich, um mit dem Attiny 2313 zu experimentieren; und die kann man rasch auf ein Breadboard stecken. Wie man hierzu vorgehen kann, ist in den Abb. 1 und 2 zu sehen; dabei wurde in Abb. 2 der USB-UART-Wandler entfernt, um dessen Verdrahtung besser sichtbar zu machen.

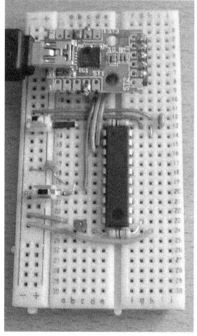 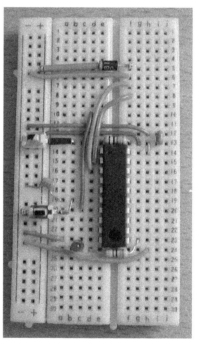

Attiny-Breadboard   *Attiny-Breadboard ohne USB-UART-Wandler*

Attiny_BB_1.jpg (112.5 KiB)   Attiny_BB_2.jpg (123.41 KiB)
337 mal betrachtet   337 mal betrachtet

Ein paar Erläuterungen zum Aufbau:
Im Norden sieht man den USB-UART-Wandler von ELV (UM 2102, nicht UM 2102N); dieser kann besonders leicht mit Steckerstiften versehen auf das Breadboard gesteckt

werden. Südwestlich davon sind der Resettaster und der Taster Ta0 (letzterer mittels Kondensator entprellt) zu sehen;Ta0 ist mit dem Eingang D.2 des Mikrocontrollers versehen und kann dort den Interrupt INT0 auslösen. Die rote LED südöstlich von dem Taster Ta0 leuchtet auf, wenn der Mikrocontroller in den Upload-Modus versetzt worden ist.

Der Mikrocontroller befindet sich im Südosten des Breadboards; damit er korrekt mit unserem Uploader-Programm arbeiten kann, muss er entsprechend eingerichtet sein (vgl. http://www.g-heinrichs.de/attiny/Erstinstallation.zip). Die Anschlüsse 22.g-j, 21.g-j, ..., 15.g-j führen zu den Ports B.0 bis B.7. Hier können z. B. LEDs oder auch unser LCD-Modul angeschlossen werden (s. Abb. 3 und 4).

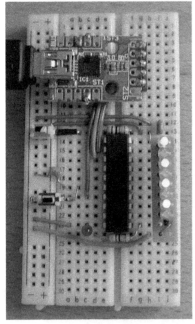 

Attiny-Breadboard mit LED-Array   Attiny-Breadboard mit LCD-Modul
Attiny_BB_3.jpg (119.04 KiB)   Attiny_BB_4.jpg (115.92 KiB)
336 mal betrachtet   336 mal betrachtet

In der Abb. 5 sind die Schaltskizzen für die Abb. 1 sowie für das LCD (Pollin-LCD) und das LED-Array (vgl. Abb. 3) angegeben.
https://www.pollin.de/bauelemente-bauteile/aktive-bauelemente/displays/
Sämtliche Fotos und Zeichnungen dieses Beitrags stammen von Ulf Ihlefeldt. Vielen Dank dafür!

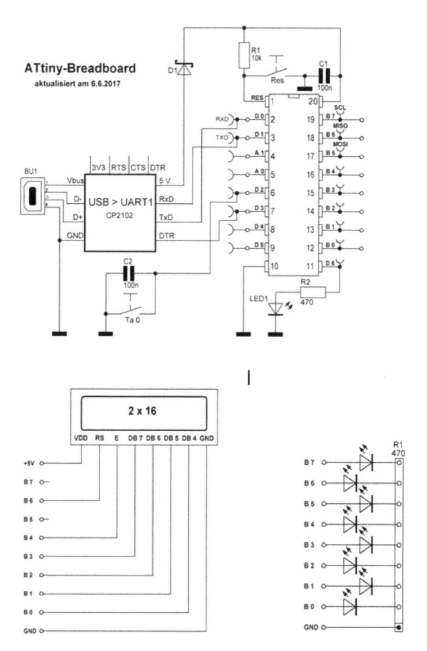

Appendix H, I, K: Circuit diagrams – Attiny_Parts – Board – Display and LEDs
BB_Schaltskizzen.jpg (44.31 KiB)

ATtiny2313

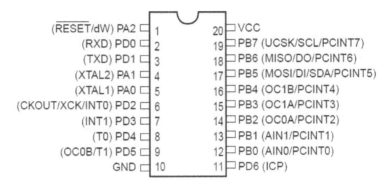

Appendix L: ATTINY pinout – Top View (source Atmel)

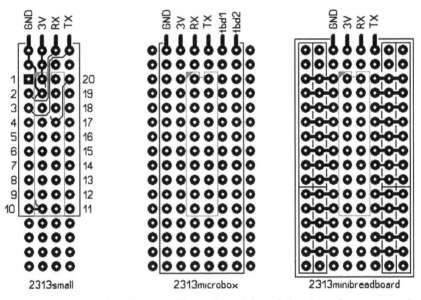

2313small   2313microbox   2313minibreadboard

Appendix M: Some PCB options – I like male and female headers plus connected via short wires on the bottom - see appendix O

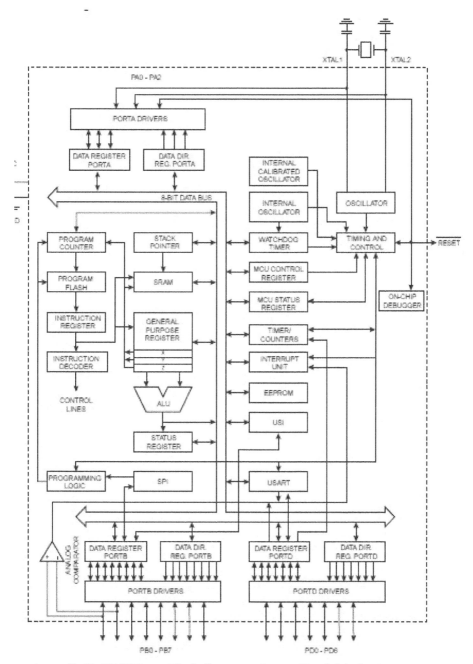

Appendix N: ATTINY 2313 Block diagram – Source Atmel datasheet

Appendix O: For a prototype system – or as well as for an application, you want to have the board on a box.

The MicroBox project done at the time used the TI MSP430 20 pin chip, https://wiki.forth-ev.de/doku.php/en:projects:microbox:start

but the same idea could apply to the MikroForth project here.

With 2 AAA batteries soldered on plus the board in a TicTac box.
There would be some prototyping space with a 2313 system and room for a connector to the outside. Connect directly or add a shield board.

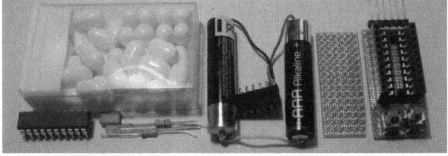

Add a bit of sticky tape and it it nearly waterproof ...

I put it under water for 6 hours – no water ingress seen afterwards.

Appendix P: Link List

to material - now mostly in German
http://www.g-heinrichs.de/wordpress/index.php/attiny/

There is as well a blog in German at
http://www.forum.g-heinrichs.de/viewforum.php?f=12

A collection of data for download and print on the Forth-ev.de website
https://wiki.forth-ev.de/doku.php/attiny

This eBook is part of the Forth Bookshelf.

The current Forth Bookshelf can be found at
https://www.amazon.co.uk/Juergen-Pintaske/e/B00N8HVEZM

Appendix Q:

Driver Installation

Blick auf die Attiny-Platine 3.0

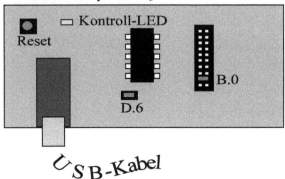

Wesentliche Bestandteile der Attiny-Platine 3.0 sind der Mikrocontroller (in der Mitte der Abb. 1) und der USB-UART-Wandler (links in der Abb. 1). Zum Betrieb der Platine muss dieser Wandler mit einem USB-Verlängerungskabel (Typ: A) mit einem PC verbunden werden.

Der USB-UART-Wandler hat dann zwei Funktionen: Zum einen versorgt er die Platine mit elektrischem Strom. Zum Anderen dient er dem Datenaustausch zwischen PC und Mi- krocontroller **Abb. 1**. Auf diese Weise können z. B. Programme vom PC auf den Mikrocontroller geladen werden.

Installation der Treiber
Der USB-UART-Wandler benötigt wie alle USB-Geräte einen Treiber. **Diese müssen auf dem PC installiert werden, bevor man die Platine mit dem PC verbindet.** Die Installation geschieht mithilfe spezieller Installationsprogramme; diese findet man auf der Seite http://www.g-heinrichs.de/wordpress/index.php/attiny/downloads/ unter dem Link "Treiber für die Platine 3.0". Nach dem Entpacken der Datei

"CP210x_VCP_Windows.zip"
findet man die beiden Installationsprogramme
CP210xVCPInstaller_x64.exe und CP210xVCPInstaller_x86.exe.

Das erste ist für neuere Rechner mit Windows (64 Bit), das zweite für ältere Rechner mit Windows (32 Bit). Falls man irrtümlich das falsche Programm startet, erfolgt eine Fehlermeldung.

Nach Beendigung des Installationsprogramms können wir die Attiny-Platine mit dem PC verbinden. Dadurch wird die Platine mit Strom versorgt und die grüne Kontroll-LED leuchtet auf. Gleichzeitig erkennt das Windows-System die neue Hardware und verknüpft sie mit den installierten Treibern. Das Ende dieses Prozesses wird in der Windows-Statuszeile angezeigt.

Testen von Soft- und Hardware

Jetzt können wir unser erstes Programm auf den Mikrocontroller hochladen. Zunächst bereiten wir die Platine vor. Dazu stecken wir in den Anschluss von PortB.0 und bei PortD.6 jeweils eine Leuchtdiode; dabei muss das lange Bein der Leuchtdioden jeweils nach links weisen.

Nun starten wir das Programm BASCOM und laden aus dem Uploader-Verzeichnis die Datei "blinken.bas". Anschließend betätigen wir die Schaltflächen "Compile Program" und "Program Chip" (vgl. Abb. 2). Dadurch wird das Programm Uploader.exe automatisch gestartet. Hier setzen wir voraus, dass BASCOM korrekt installiert und für unser Uploader-Programm entsprechend vorbereitet wurde; passende Anweisungen dazu findet man auf der oben genannten Download-Seite.

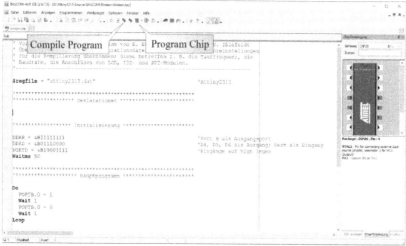

Abb. 2:

Im Uploader-Programm sehen wir links den Maschinencode von blinken.bas. Er wurde automatisch von BASCOM als HEX-Datei an das Uploader-Programm übergeben; deswegen brauchen wir die Schaltfläche "Hex-Datei öffnen" auch nicht mehr betätigen.

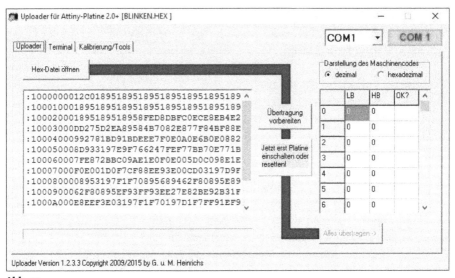

Abb. 3:

Auf der rechten Seite wählen wir nun die COM-Nummer des USB-UART-Wandlers aus und betätigen dann die Schaltfläche "Übertragung vorbereiten".
Anschließend drücken wir kurz den roten Reset-Taster auf der Attiny-Platine. Nun leuchtet die LED bei PortD.6 auf; dies ist ein Zeichen dafür, dass der Mikrocontroller den Bootloader gestartet hat. Dabei handelt es sich um ein kleines Programm, welches den Maschinencode vom PC entgegen nehmen und im Programmspeicher des Mikrocontrollers ablegen kann.

Schließlich betätigen wir im Uploader die Schaltfläche "Alles übertragen". Jetzt erlischt die LED bei Port D.6 und ein Balken am unteren Rand des Programmfensters zeigt den Fortschritt an. Wenn die Übertragung korrekt abgelaufen ist, wird dies durch einen grünen Haken neben der Übertragen-Schaltfläche angezeigt.
Sollte das Uploader-Programm Probleme bei der Übertragung feststellen (was hoffentlich nicht der Fall sein wird), zeigt es dies durch eine entsprechende Fehlermeldung an. Hier einige Hinweise zur Fehlerbehebung:

- Ist die richtige Schnittstelle aktiviert? Ein grünes COM-Signal heißt nicht automatisch, dass die richtige Schnittstelle ausgesucht wurde. Gegebenenfalls versucht man die Übertragung noch einmal mit einer anderen COM-Nummer.

- Ist der Bootloader korrekt gestartet worden?

- Erlischt die LED bei Port D.6 nicht oder meldet der Uploader einen Timeout-Fehler, wenn die Schaltfläche "Alles übertragen" betätigt wurde, so weist dies auf Probleme bei den Signalleitungen RXD und TXD hin.

- Geht die LED bei Port D.6 aus und treten trotzdem Probleme bei der Übertragung auf, könnte dies an einer unzureichenden Kalibrierung des Oszillators beim Attiny liegen. Wie man hier für Abhilfe sorgen kann, kann man im Kapitel "Kalibrierung des Attiny" nachlesen.

Während der Übertragung wird jedes einzelne Byte vom Attiny quittiert; d. h. der Attiny sendet jedes empfangene Byte an den Uploader zurück und der vergleicht es mit dem gesendeten Byte. Wenn hier Abweichungen auftreten, wird dies durch einen rot durchgestrichenen IC neben der Übertragen-Schaltfläche angezeigt. Auch in diesem Fall sollten die obigen Hinweise zur Fehlerbehebung beachtet werden.

Wir gehen jetzt davon aus, dass die Übertragung reibungslos funktioniert hat. In diesem Fall startet der Attiny unmittelbar nach der Übertragung automatisch das Blink-Programm: Die LED am Port B.0 sollte jetzt blinken.

Wir schließen jetzt den Uploader und trennen die Platine vom PC: Die grüne Kontroll-LED geht aus und das Blinken hört auf. Nach einer Weile (ca. 10 Sekunden) schließen wir die Platine wieder an den PC an und versorgen sie dadurch wieder mit Strom: Die grüne Kontroll-LED geht an und der Mikrocontroller startet sein Blink-Programm. Test erfolgreich bestanden? Dann ...

...Gratulation!

Appendix R:

Das Attiny-Projekt ✕ *MikroForth einstellen*

MikroForth einstellen

MikroForth erlaubt folgende Anpassungen

1. Programm zum Uploaden
2. Warnhinweis bei Überschreiben von Wörtern
3. Auswahl des Separators in der Adressenzuweisungstabelle
4. Anzeigen der Adressen im HEX- oder Dezimalformat

Die entsprechenden Einstellungen sind inder Datei forth2.ini gespeichert. Sie können dort bei Bedarf mit einem Editor geändert werden.

Programm zum Uploaden

Soll auf das Programm "Uploader.exe" zurückgegriffen werden, besteht der Eintrag in der iniDatei einfach aus einem Minuszeichen:

externuploader=-

Ansonsten wird hinter das Gleichheitszeichen der Name des gewünschten Programms mitsamt dem vollständigen Pfad angegeben.

Warnhinweis bei Überschreiben von Wörtern

Häufig müssen einzelne Wörter des aktuellen Vokabulars überschrieben werden. Ist der Eintrag

ueberschreiben=1

dann gibt MikroForth einen entsprechender Warnhinweis in einem Meldungsfenster. Sie haben dann die Möglichkeit, das Überschreiben zu unterbinden. Wenn Sie den Wert 0 hinter das Gleichheitszeichen schreiben, dann erfolgt nur ein Hinweis im Statusbereich und das alte Wort wird überschrieben.

Sie können diesen Parameter auch über Bearbeiten - Einstellungen ändern.

Auswahl des Separators in der Adressenzuweisungstabelle

In der Adresszuweisungstabelle befindet sich zwischen dem Forth-Wort und der zugehörigen

Adresse ein so genannter **Separator**. Standardmäßig ist dies ein Doppel-Größer-Zeichen mit dem ASCII-Code 187. Sie können dieses Zeichen in der Zeile

separator=187

ändern. Geben Sie dazu hinter demGleichheitszeichen einen anderen Code ein. Dieser Code darf aber nicht zu einem Zeichen gehören, das im Namen eines Forth-Wortes auftaucht. Daher empfiehlt es sich, nur ASCII-Codes oberhalb von 127 zu benutzen.

Anzeigen der Adressen im HEX- oder Dezimalformat

Sie können auswählen, ob die Adressen im Hex- oder im Dezimalformat angezeigt werden sollen. Dazu wird die Zeile

hexadressen=1

benutzt. Bei dem Eintrag 1 werden die Adressen im HEX-Format angezeigt, bei dem Eintrag 0 in dezimaler Schreibweise.

Sie können diesen Parameter auch über Bearbeiten - Einstellungen ändern.

Appendix S:

Mini-Oszi mit Attiny2313 und OLED

by wordpress · Leave a Comment

Mit Hilfe eines kleinen OLEDs und eines AD-Wandlers kann man ein kleines Digital-Oszilloskop bauen. Mehr dazu finden Sie hier.

Mini-Oszi mit OLED SSD1306 und PCF8591-Modul

Beitrag von Heinrichs » Do 1. Dez 2016, 13:14

Für ca. 4 bis 10 Euro kann man OLED-Displays mit einer Diagonalen von ca. 1 Zoll und 128*64 Pixeln erwerben. Sie benötigen eine Spannungsversorgung von 3,3 V - 5,0 V und werden über I2C, manchmal auch zusätzlich über SPI, angesteuert.

OLED SSD1306 foto_oled.jpg (13.99 KiB) siehe oben rechts
Ein solches Modul können wir direkt an die Buchsenleiste unserer Attiny-Platine anschließen (vgl. Abb.). Das Modul steht dann zwar auf dem Kopf, aber es lässt sich so initialisieren, dass die Bildausgabe ein aufrechtes Bild erzeugt. VCC verbinden wir mit dem 3,3-V-Anschluss neben dem USB-COM-Wandler, GND schließen wir an Masse an, SCL und SDA werden mit PortB.7 bzw. PortB.5 verbunden. Auf dem Modul befinden sich schon passende Pull-Up-Widerstände; deswegen können wir auf die I2C-Pull-Up-Jumper bei unserer Attiny-Platine verzichten.

Auf diesem OLED-Modul werden wir unser Spannungsdiagramm anzeigen. Zusätzlich benötigen wir noch einen AD-Wandler; dazu soll ein PCF8591-Modul zum Einsatz kommen, wie es hier schon beschrieben worden ist.

Nun zur Programmierung: Das SSD1306-Modul ist recht komplex; das zugehörige Manual umfasst 65 Seiten. Für den arduino gibt es passende Libraries, ebenso für den BASCOM-Compiler. Leider funktioniert die BASCOM-Library "glcdSSD1306-I2C.lib" nicht mit der frei erhältlichen Demo-Version von BASCOM. Außerdem belegen diese Libraries mehr Speicherplatz, als der Attiny2313 zur Verfügung hat. Deswegen habe ich für mein Mini-Oszi-Programm auf die grundlegenden I2C-Befehle zurückgegriffen. Diese findet man im Manual auf den Seiten 28ff.

Wie üblich muss der Baustein zunächst adressiert werden; die Schreibadresse lautet bei meinem Modul: &H78. Danach erwartet der Baustein Kontroll-Bytes oder Daten-Bytes; erstere stellen Befehle und zugehörige Parameter dar, letztere sind die eigentlichen Bilddaten und werden direkt in das Graphik-RAM geschrieben. Wie kann das Modul nun diese beiden Typen unterscheiden? Dazu wertet es die ersten beiden Bits (von links aus gezählt) aus, vgl. Manual S. 20:

Das erste Bit (MSB) ist das sogenannte Co-Bit; hat dieses continuation-Bit den Wert 1, so erwartet das Modul nur noch ein einziges Byte. Hat das Bit den Wert 0, so erwartet es einen ganzen Datenstrom.

Das nächste Bit (MSB-1) ist das sogenannte D/C#-Bit; hat dieses data/command-select-Bit den Wert 1, wird / werden das nächste Byte / die nächsten Bytes als Daten-Bytes gedeutet, ansonsten als Kontroll-Bytes.

Beispiele:

Der Befehl &H 00 = &B 0000 0000 zeigt dem SSD1306, dass ein Strom von Kontroll-Bytes folgt.
Der Befehl &H 81 = &B 1000 0001 (Einstellung des Kontrastes) hat das Co-Bit 1 und das D/C#-Bit 0; das Modul erwartet demnach genau ein weiteres Byte, und zwar ein Kontroll-Byte. In diesem Fall ist es der Kontrast-Wert.

Der Befehl &H 40 = &B 0100 0000 zeigt dem SSD1306, dass es sich bei folgenden Bytes um Daten-Bytes handelt, die in den Grafik-RAM geschrieben werden sollen.

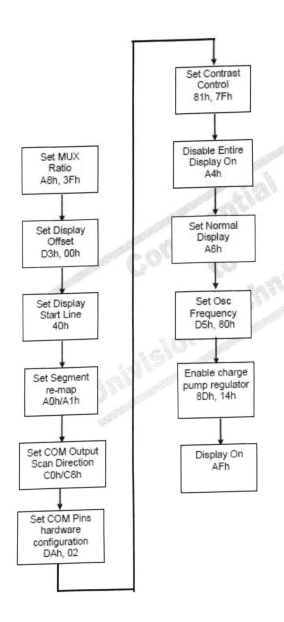

Byte-Ströme werden durch einen I2c-Stop-Befehl beendet.

Zu Beginn muss das Display initialisiert werden. Glücklicherweise findet man auf der vorletzten Seite des Manuals (S. 64) eine Beispiel-Sequenz für die Initialisierung.

Beispielsequenz für die Initialisierung
initialisierung_flussdiagramm.jpg (28.67 KiB) 1494 mal betrachtet

Diese Sequenz musste ich nur in einigen wenigen Punkten modifizieren, u. A. um das Bild vertikal zu spiegeln. Im Quellcode (s. u.) findet man die einzelnen Kommandos auch stichwortartig kommentiert. Diese Kommentare stammen zum Teil aus Programmen von I. Dobson und Sonal Pinto.

Wie spricht man nun die einzelnen Pixel des Displays an? Dazu greift man auf das Grafik-RAM des Displays zurück. Dieses ist Byte-weise strukturiert: Jeweils 1 Byte entsprechen 8 senkrecht untereinander angeordneten Pixel. Der Pixelwert 1 entsprecht einem leuchtenden Punkt auf dem Display. In der folgenden Abbildung sind die Pixel eines solchen Bytes hell braun gefärbt.

Die Position eines solchen Sprites ist horizontal durch den Segment-Wert gekennzeichnet und vertikal durch den Page-Wert. Ein einziges Pixel wird damit durch die Angabe dreier Werte bestimmt: den Segment-Wert, den Page-Wert und die Bit-Nummer. Soll das 2-Pixel-Muster aus der Abbildung angezeigt werden, dann muss das Byte &B 0100 0100 = &H 44 in die Page 3 des Segments 14 geschrieben werden. Dazu übermittelt man dem Modul zunächst Page-Wert und Segmentwert für das Sprite und dann dessen Wert (vgl. Source-Code).

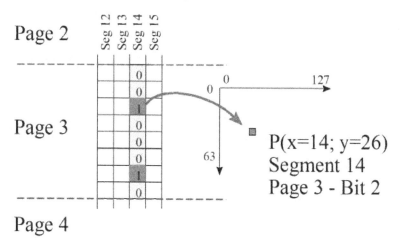

Grafik-RAM
grafik_ram_klein.jpg (22.55 KiB)

Will man z. B. das Display löschen, muss das komplette Grafik-RAM mit Nullen gefüllt werden. In diesem Fall muss dem Modul lediglich zu Beginn die Startposition (Segemnet0, Page0) übertragen werden; das Modul inkrementiert den Sprite-Zeiger automatisch, jedesmal wenn ein Sprite-Wert übertragen worden ist.

Code: Alles auswählen

```
' Datei für Attiny-Platine von E. Eube, G. Heinrichs und U. Ihlefeldt
' Über die zu zugehörige Konfigurationsdatei werden automatisch Voreinstellungen
' für die Kompilierung übernommen; diese betreffen z. B. die Taktfrequenz, die
' Baudrate, die Anschlüsse von LCD, I2C- und SPI-Modulen.

' Programm nach I. Dobson und Sonal Pinto
' OLED display 128x64 using SSD1306 0.96"
' PCF8591-Modul Typ Y0027

' SCL -> B.7
' SDA -> B.5

' Ta0: Messintervall kleiner, d. h. Aufzeichnung schneller;
' Maximale Schnelligkeit: ca. 1 Durchlauf (128 Messsungen) in ca. 210 ms
' Ta1: Messintervall größer
' Ta0 und Ta1 gleichzeitig betätigt: Messung stoppen
' Reset-Taster: Neu-Start

'-------------------------------------------------------------------
---

$regfile = "attiny2313.dat" 'Dadurch wird auch das Pin Layout bestimmt


'*********************************************************
'******************** Deklarationen *********************

Declare Sub Zeichne_punkt
Declare Sub Init_oled
Declare Sub Loeschen_oled
Declare Function Analogwert_von_pcf_modul() As Byte
Dim X As Byte
Dim X0 As Byte
```

```
Dim X1 As Byte
Dim Y As Byte
Dim Y0 As Byte
Dim Y1 As Byte
Dim Punkt As Byte
Dim I As Word
Dim Kontrast As Byte
Dim Send As Byte
Dim Write_adresse_pcf As Byte
Dim Read_adresse_pcf As Byte
Dim K As Byte
Dim Messwert As Byte
Dim Messintervall As Byte
Dim Ende As Byte
Dim Write_adresse_oled As Byte


'***********************************************************
'***************** Initialisierung *********************

Ddrb = &B11111111        'Port B als Ausgangsport
Ddrd = &B01110000         'D4, D5, D6 als Ausgang; Rest als Eingang
Portd = &B10001111           'Eingänge auf high legen

Config I2cdelay = 1           'I2C-Taktung möglichst rasch

Enable Int0                 'vgl. BASCOM-Hilfe...
Config Int0 = Falling
Enable Int1          'Achtung: T1 ist im Gegensatz zu T0 nicht
                     'mit einem Kondensator entprellt
Config Int1 = Falling
Enable Interrupts
On Int0 Schneller
On Int1 Langsamer

Kontrast = 200                    'hoher Kontrast
Write_adresse_pcf = 144            'PCF8591
Read_adresse_pcf = 145
Write_adresse_oled = &H78          'OLED SSD1306
Messintervall = 20        'Wartezeit nach jeder Messung (in ms)
```

```
Waitms 50                   'warte bis Kondensator bei Ta0 geladen

'********************************************************
'******************* Hauptprogramm ********************

Call Init_oled
Call Loeschen_oled
Do
  For X = 0 To 127
    Disable Interrupts       'Ausführen der Interruptroutine nicht
                    'während einer Messung
    Y = Analogwert_von_pcf_modul()
    Y = Y / 4               'Analogwert [0..255] -> Anzeigewert [0..63]
    Call Zeichne_punkt
    Waitms Messintervall
    Ende = Pind.2 + Pind.3       'Ende = 0, wenn Ta0 und Ta1
                    ' gleichzeitig betätigt werden
    If Ende = 0 Then X = 127     'und dann ggf. Schleifenabbruch
    Enable Interrupts
  Next X
  If Ende > 0 Then Call Loeschen_oled
Loop Until Ende = 0
End


'********************************************************
'******************* Unterprogramme ********************

Sub Init_oled
'(
  I2cstart                   'OLED da?
  I2cwbyte Write_adresse_oled
  If Err = 0 Then Portd.6 = 1    'LED bei D.6 an, wenn OLED gefunden
  I2cstop
  Waitms 200
  Portd.6 = 0
')
  I2cstart
  I2cwbyte Write_adresse_oled
```

```
I2cwbyte &H00              'Command Stream nötig

I2cwbyte &HAE               'DISPLAYOFF

I2cwbyte &HD5                        'SETDISPLAYCLOCKDIV
I2cwbyte &H80              'ratio 0x80

I2cwbyte &HA8              'Set MUX
I2cwbyte &H3F              '&H1F for 128x32; &H3F for 128x64

I2cwbyte &HD3                        'SETDISPLAYOFFSET
I2cwbyte &H00

I2cwbyte &H40                        'SETSTARTLINE

I2cwbyte &H8D              'CHARGEPUMP
I2cwbyte &H14              'vccstate 14 for chargepump

I2cwbyte &H20              'MEMORYMODE
I2cwbyte &H00              'horizontal addr mode

I2cwbyte &HA0              'SEGREMAP links–rechts A0/A1

I2cwbyte &HC8              'COMSCANDEC (&HC0 vert. gespieg.)

I2cwbyte &HDA                       'SETCOMPINS
I2cwbyte &H12                       '&H12 for 64 rows

I2cwbyte &H81                       'SETCONTRAST
I2cwbyte Kontrast                   'value 1-->256

I2cwbyte &HD9                        'SETPRECHARGE
I2cwbyte &HF1              'vccstate  F1

I2cwbyte &HDB                       'SETVCOMDETECT
I2cwbyte &H30              '&H30 -> 0.83*VCC;

I2cwbyte &HA4                        'DISPLAYALLON_RESUME

I2cwbyte &HA6                        'NORMALDISPLAY
```

```
    I2cwbyte &HAF                          'Display on
    I2cstop
End Sub


Sub Zeichne_punkt
'  x zwischen 0 und 127
'  y zwischen 0 und 63

    Y0 = Y Mod 8
    Y1 = Y / 8
    Y1 = Y1 + &HB0
    I2cstart
    I2cwbyte Write_adresse_oled
    I2cwbyte &H80                          'Single Command
    I2cwbyte Y1          'Page (Y) &HB0 = Col0 entspricht Zeile
    I2cstop

    X0 = X Mod 16
    X1 = X / 16
    X1 = X1 + &H10
    I2cstart
    I2cwbyte Write_adresse_oled
    I2cwbyte &H00                          'command stream
    I2cwbyte X0                     'Spalte x Low Nibble
    I2cwbyte X1                     'Spalte x High Nibble
    I2cstop

    Punkt = 0
    Punkt.y0 = 1
    I2cstart
    I2cwbyte Write_adresse_oled
    I2cwbyte &HC0                          '1 Datum
    I2cwbyte Punkt       'Sprite aus 7 inaktiven und einem aktiven
' Pixel: vertikal z. B. 00000100
    I2cstop
End Sub


Sub Loeschen_oled
    I2cstart
```

```
I2cwbyte Write_adresse_oled
I2cwbyte &H80                      'Single Command
I2cwbyte &HB0                      'Page (Y) &HB0 = Col0
I2cstop

I2cstart
I2cwbyte Write_adresse_oled
I2cwbyte &H00                      'command stream
I2cwbyte &H00                      'Select start (X) column 0
I2cwbyte &H10
I2cstop

I2cstart
I2cwbyte Write_adresse_oled
I2cwbyte &H40                      'Datenstrom für das RAM
For I = 0 To 1023
  I2cwbyte 0
Next I
I2cstop
End Sub


Function Analogwert_von_pcf_modul() As Byte
' knr=0 -> ldr, knr=3  -> poti, knr=1 -> temperatur (Modul-Typ YL-04))
' knr 1 -> poti, knr 3 -> ldr, knr 2 -> temperatur
' (Modul-Typ Mini: Y0027; Aktoren u. Sensoren in einer Reihe; große LED)
 K = 3                             'LDR bei Y0027
 I2cstart
 I2cwbyte Write_adresse_pcf
 I2cwbyte K
 Waitus 10
 I2cstop
 Waitus 10


' Messung
 I2cstart
 I2cwbyte Read_adresse_pcf
 I2crbyte Messwert , Nack
 I2cstop
 Waitus 10
 Analogwert_von_pcf_modul = Messwert
```

End Function


```
'*******************************************************
'******************Interruptroutinen********************

Schneller:                'Sprung-Marke, kein Subroutine-Name
 If Messintervall > 1 Then Messintervall = Messintervall - 2     'Messintervall nicht
unter 0
Return

Langsamer:
 If Messintervall < 250 Then Messintervall = Messintervall + 10
 ' Waitms 10
Return


'*******************************************************
' Bemerkung: Da T1 nicht entprellt ist, wird durch
' eine einzige Betätigung von
' T1 ggf. mehrfach ein int1-Interrupt ausgelöst.
' Durch wenige Tastendrücke bei T1
' ist das Lauflicht auf Minimaltempo gebracht.
' Dem Prellen kann z. B. durch eine Pause (ca. 10 ms)
' in der int1-Interrupt-Routine
' begegnet werden.
```


Das Programm erfasst die Spannungswerte an einem der Eingänge des PCF-Module (hier Kanal 3) und stellt sie grafisch auf dem Display an. Die Zeitbasis kann dabei mir den Tastern Ta0 und Ta1 verändert werden. Drückt man beide Taster gleichzeitig, wird die Messung angehalten. Mit dem Reset-Taster kann dann eine neue Messung eingeleitet werden. Im Anhang findet man ein Video dazu.

Re: Mini-Oszi mit OLED SSD1306 und PCF8591-Modul
Beitrag von Heinrichs » Di 20. Dez 2016, 11:54

Neben den OLEDs mit dem Treiber SSD1306 werden auch OLEDs angeboten, welche äußerlich von den SSD1306-OLEDs nicht zu unterscheiden sind (zumal da das eigentliche Display dasselbe ist), aber einen anderen Treiber besitzen, nämlich den Treiber SSH1106. Dieser Treiber arbeitet ganz ähnlich wie der SSD1306, aber er besitzt ein RAM mit einer 132x64-Struktur. Das bedeutet, dass die Spaltenanzahl des Treibers nicht mit der Spaltenanzahl des Displays übereinstimmt. Will man die Spalte x des Displays ansteuern, muss man beim SSH1106 den Index $x+2$ benutzen.

Auch bei der Autoinkrementierung gibt es einen Unterschied: Diese funktioniert beim SSD1306 PAGE-übergreifend, beim SSH1106 aber nicht; hier muss jede PAGE neu adressiert werden. Am Beispiel des Löschens soll dies verdeutlicht werden:
Code: Alles auswählen

```
Sub Loeschen_oled_SSD1306
  I2cstart
  I2cwbyte Write_adresse_oled
  I2cwbyte &H80              'Single Command
  I2cwbyte &HB0              'Page (Y) &HB0 = Col0
  I2cstop

  I2cstart
  I2cwbyte Write_adresse_oled
  I2cwbyte &H00              'command stream
  I2cwbyte &H00              'Select start (X) column 0
  I2cwbyte &H10
```

```
  I2cstop

  I2cstart
  I2cwbyte Write_adresse_oled
  I2cwbyte &H40              'Datenstrom für das RAM
  For I = 0 To 1023
    I2cwbyte 0
  Next I
  I2cstop
End Sub


Sub Loeschen_oled_SSH1106
  For X0 = 0 To 7
  X1 = &HB0 + X0
  I2cstart
  I2cwbyte Write_adresse_oled
  I2cwbyte &H80                 'Single Command
  I2cwbyte X1              'Page (Y) &HB0 = Col0
  I2cstop

  I2cstart
  I2cwbyte Write_adresse_oled
  I2cwbyte &H00                'command stream
  I2cwbyte &H02      'Select start column 0; offset 2
  I2cwbyte &H10
  I2cstop

  I2cstart
  I2cwbyte Write_adresse_oled
  I2cwbyte &H40              'Datenstrom für das RAM
  For X = 0 To 127
    I2cwbyte 0
  Next X
  I2cstop
  Next X0
End Sub
```

Im Handling ist das SSH1106-OLED sicherlich etwas sperriger; dafür ist es aber - insbesondere in der 1.3"-Variante - deutlich preisgünstiger.

APP T: Word List File: For now, only as original in German, slightly edited

[Wortliste] ========================= Overview

wort0=+
wort1=.
wort2=<
wort3=>
wort4=and
wort5=begin
wort6=blink
wort7=DDBitB
wort8=do
wort9=drop
wort10=dup
wort11=end
wort12=equal
wort13=com>
wort14=eprom>
wort15=getOSCCAL
wort16=I
wort17=i2cread
wort18=i2cstart
wort19=i2cstop
wort20=i2cwrite
wort21=init
wort22=initCom
wort23=initInt0
wort24=initInt1
wort25=inPortB
wort26=loop
wort27=main
wort28=or
wort29=outPortB
wort30=popreg
wort31=pushreg
wort32=reti
wort33=rot
wort34=sei
wort35=setOSCCAL
wort36=skipIF
wort37=stackInit
wort38=swap
wort39=>com
wort40=>eprom
wort41=until
wort42=wait
wort43=wait1ms

wort44=waitms
wort45=wdogOff
wort46=xor
wort47=int0
wort48=int1
wort49=-
wort50=*
wort51=DDRB
wort52=over
wort53==>R
wort54=R>
wort55=T0?
wort56=T1?
wort57=DDBitD
wort58=DDRD
wort59=InPortD
wort60=/
wort61=outPortD
wort62=not
wort63=t1Capt
wort64=t1CompA
wort65=t1Ovf
wort66=t0Ovf
wort67=usart0Rx
wort68=usart0Udre
wort69=usart0Tx
wort70=analogComp
wort71=pCInt
wort72=t1CompB
wort73=t0CompA
wort74=t0CompB
wort75=usiStart
wort76=usiOvf
wort77=eeReady
wort78=wdtOvf
wort79==>sram
wort80=sram>
wort81=toggleB
wort82=initt0ovf
wort83=setTimer0
Anzahl=84

[+] ===================================== 0 +
Typ=A
ParamAnzahl=5
KomAnzahl=3
Parameter0=$0E91
Parameter1=$1E91
Parameter2=$010F
Parameter3=$0D93
Parameter4=$0895
Zeile0=(a b -- erg)
Zeile1=
Zeile2=erg = a + b

[.] ===================================== 1 .
Typ=A
ParamAnzahl=5
KomAnzahl=5
Parameter0=$1FEF
Parameter1=$0E91
Parameter2=$17BB
Parameter3=$08BB
Parameter4=$0895
Zeile0=(a --)
Zeile1=
Zeile2=Gibt a auf Port B aus;
Zeile3=(Datenrichtungsbits von Port B werden
Zeile4=alle auf 1gesetzt.)

[<] ===================================== 2 <
Typ=A
ParamAnzahl=8
KomAnzahl=6
Parameter0=$21E0
Parameter1=$1E91
Parameter2=$0E91
Parameter3=$0117
Parameter4=$08F0
Parameter5=$20E0
Parameter6=$2D93
Parameter7=$0895
Zeile0=(a b -- flag)
Zeile1=
Zeile2=Beispiel: a b <
Zeile3=
Zeile4=Legt 1 (TRUE) auf den Stack,
Zeile5=wenn a < b ist, sonst 0.

[>] ===================================== 3 >
Typ=F
ParamAnzahl=2
KomAnzahl=6
Parameter0=SWAP
Parameter1=<
Zeile0=(a b -- flag)
Zeile1=
Zeile2=Beispiel: a b >
Zeile3=
Zeile4=Legt 1 (TRUE) auf den Stack,
Zeile5=wenn a > b ist, sonst 0.

[and] ================================ 4 and
Typ=A
ParamAnzahl=5
KomAnzahl=3
Parameter0=$0E91
Parameter1=$1E91
Parameter2=$0123
Parameter3=$0D93
Parameter4=$0895
Zeile0=(a b -- erg)
Zeile1=
Zeile2=erg = a and b

[begin] ============================== 5 begin
Typ=A
ParamAnzahl=7
KomAnzahl=8
Parameter0=$0F91
Parameter1=$1F91
Parameter2=$1F93
Parameter3=$0F93
Parameter4=$1F93
Parameter5=$0F93
Parameter6=$0895
Zeile0=(--)
Zeile1=
Zeile2=Beispiel: BEGIN Bef1 Bef2 ... Befn UNTIL
Zeile3=
Zeile4=Wiederholt die Befehle Bef1, Bef2, ...,
Zeile5=Befn, bis UNTIL auf TOS = 1 stößt
Zeile6=
Zeile7=s. a. UNTIL

[blink] ============================= 6 blink
Typ=F
ParamAnzahl=7
KomAnzahl=8
Parameter0=SWAP
Parameter1=.
Parameter2=DUP
Parameter3=WAITMS
Parameter4=0
Parameter5=.
Parameter6=WAITMS
Zeile0=(b hp --)
Zeile1=
Zeile2=Beispiel: b hp blink
Zeile3=
Zeile4=Gibt Bitmuster b auf Port B aus,
Zeile5=wartet hp (halbe Periode) Millisekunden,
Zeile6=gibt 0 auf Port B aus und wartet wieder
Zeile7=hp Millisekunden

[DDBitB] =========================== 7 DDBitB
Typ=A
ParamAnzahl=19
KomAnzahl=7
Parameter0=$3E91
Parameter1=$1E91
Parameter2=$27B3
Parameter3=$07E0
Parameter4=$1023
Parameter5=$01E0
Parameter6=$1030
Parameter7=$19F0
Parameter8=$000F
Parameter9=$1A95
Parameter10=$FBCF
Parameter11=$3030
Parameter12=$11F0
Parameter13=$202B
Parameter14=$02C0
Parameter15=$0095
Parameter16=$2023
Parameter17=$27BB
Parameter18=$0895
Zeile0=(bit flag --)
Zeile1=

Zeile2=Beispiel : bit flag DDBitB
Zeile3=
Zeile4=Setzt den Anschluss bit des Ports B
Zeile5=als Ausgang, wenn flag = 1,
Zeile6=sonst als Eingang.

[do] =================================== 8 do
Typ=A
ParamAnzahl=11
KomAnzahl=14
Parameter0=$2E91
Parameter1=$3E91
Parameter2=$0F91
Parameter3=$1F91
Parameter4=$1F93
Parameter5=$0F93
Parameter6=$3F93
Parameter7=$2F93
Parameter8=$1F93
Parameter9=$0F93
Parameter10=$0895
Zeile0=(n i --)
Zeile1=
Zeile2=Beispiel: n i DO Bef1 Bef2 ... Befn LOOP
Zeile3=
Zeile4=Wiederholt die Befehle Bef1, Bef2, ...,
Zeile5=Befn; die Schleife beginnt mit dem Index
Zeile6=i und läuft bis n (einschließlich). Die
Zeile7=Schleife wird mindestens einmal
Zeile8=durchlaufen. Innerhalb der Schleife kann
Zeile9=durch das Wort I auf den Index
Zeile10=zurückgegriffen werden.
Zeile11=
Zeile12=s. a. LOOP
Zeile13=s. a. I

[drop] ============================== 9 drop
Typ=A
ParamAnzahl=2
KomAnzahl=3
Parameter0=$0E91
Parameter1=$0895
Zeile0=(n --)
Zeile1=
Zeile2=Entfernt den TOS

[dup] ============================== 10 dup
Typ=A
ParamAnzahl=4
KomAnzahl=3
Parameter0=$0E91
Parameter1=$0D93
Parameter2=$0D93
Parameter3=$0895
Zeile0=(n -- n n)
Zeile1=
Zeile2=Dupliziert den TOS

[end] ============================== 11 end
Typ=A
ParamAnzahl=1
KomAnzahl=5
Parameter0=$FFCF
Zeile0=(--)
Zeile1=
Zeile2=Führt eine Endlosleerschleife aus;
Zeile3=wird für das Ende eines Programms
Zeile4=empfohlen.

[equal] ========================== 12 equal
Typ=A
ParamAnzahl=8
KomAnzahl=6
Parameter0=$21E0
Parameter1=$1E91
Parameter2=$0E91
Parameter3=$0117
Parameter4=$09F0
Parameter5=$20E0
Parameter6=$2D93
Parameter7=$0895
Zeile0=(a b -- flag)
Zeile1=
Zeile2=Beispiel: a b EQUAL
Zeile3=
Zeile4=Legt 1 (TRUE) auf den Stack,
Zeile5=wenn a = b ist, sonst 0 (FALSE).

[com>] ============================== 13 com>
Typ=A
ParamAnzahl=5
KomAnzahl=7
Parameter0=$5F9B
Parameter1=$FECF
Parameter2=$0CB1
Parameter3=$0D93
Parameter4=$0895
Zeile0=(-- n)
Zeile1=
Zeile2=Legt über COM-Schnittstelle empfangenes
Zeile3=Byte auf Stack.
Zeile4=
Zeile5=s. a. >COM
Zeile6=s. a. INITCOM

[eprom>] =========================== 14 eprom>
Typ=A
ParamAnzahl=8
KomAnzahl=5
Parameter0=$0E91
Parameter1=$E199
Parameter2=$FECF
Parameter3=$0EBB
Parameter4=$E09A
Parameter5=$1DB3
Parameter6=$1D93
Parameter7=$0895
Zeile0=(a -- w)
Zeile1=
Zeile2=Liest den Wert w aus der
Zeile3=EEPROM-Adresse a und legt ihn auf
Zeile4=den Stack

[getOSCCAL] ===================== 15 getOSCCAL
Typ=A
ParamAnzahl=3
KomAnzahl=3
Parameter0=$01B7
Parameter1=$0D93
Parameter2=$0895
Zeile0=(-- n)
Zeile1=
Zeile2=Legt den OSCCAL-Wert auf den Stack.

[I] ==================================== 16 I

Typ=A

ParamAnzahl=8

KomAnzahl=6

Parameter0=$4F91

Parameter1=$5F91

Parameter2=$2F91

Parameter3=$2F93

Parameter4=$5F93

Parameter5=$4F93

Parameter6=$2D93

Parameter7=$0895

Zeile0=(-- i)

Zeile1=

Zeile2=Legt den Schleifenindex i einer

Zeile3=DO-LOOP-Schleife auf den Stack.

Zeile4=Darf nur zwischen DO und LOOP

Zeile5=auftauchen.

[i2cread] ======================= 17 i2cread]

Typ=A

ParamAnzahl=37

KomAnzahl=5

Parameter0=$38E0

Parameter1=$00E0

Parameter2=$1E91

Parameter3=$07D0

Parameter4=$000F

Parameter5=$022B

Parameter6=$3A95

Parameter7=$D9F7

Parameter8=$0DD0

Parameter9=$0D93

Parameter10=$0895

Parameter11=$21E0

Parameter12=$BD98

Parameter13=$12D0

Parameter14=$C79A

Parameter15=$B59B

Parameter16=$20E0

Parameter17=$0ED0

Parameter18=$C798

Parameter19=$0CD0

Parameter20=$BD9A

Parameter21=$0895

Parameter22=$C59A

Parameter23=$1030
Parameter24=$09F4
Parameter25=$C598
Parameter26=$05D0
Parameter27=$C79A
Parameter28=$03D0
Parameter29=$C798
Parameter30=$01D0
Parameter31=$0895
Parameter32=$88EE
Parameter33=$93E0
Parameter34=$0197
Parameter35=$F1F7
Parameter36=$0895
Zeile0=(ACK -- Wert)
Zeile1=
Zeile2=Ein Wert wird vom Slave gelesen;
Zeile3=wenn ACK = 0 ist, wird ein
Zeile4=Acknowledge-Signal gegeben.

[i2cstart] ===================== 18 i2cstart
Typ=A
ParamAnzahl=7
KomAnzahl=4
Parameter0=$C598
Parameter1=$88EE
Parameter2=$93E0
Parameter3=$0197
Parameter4=$F1F7
Parameter5=$C798
Parameter6=$0895
Zeile0=(--)
Zeile1=
Zeile2=Startsignal für I2C-Bus wird gesendet
Zeile3=(SDA von 1 auf 0; dann SCL von 1 auf 0).

[i2cstop] ======================= 19 i2cstop
Typ=A
ParamAnzahl=9
KomAnzahl=6
Parameter0=$BF9A
Parameter1=$BD9A
Parameter2=$C59A
Parameter3=$C79A
Parameter4=$88EE
Parameter5=$93E0

Parameter6=$0197
Parameter7=$F1F7
Parameter8=$0895
Zeile0=(--)
Zeile1=
Zeile2=Initialisiert den I2C-Bus (SCL und
Zeile3=SDA auf 1); Datenrichtungsbits für
Zeile4=SDA (PortB.5) und SCL (PortB.7)
Zeile5=werden gesetzt.

[i2cwrite] ===================== 20 i2cwrite
Typ=A
ParamAnzahl=34
KomAnzahl=5
Parameter0=$38E0
Parameter1=$0E91
Parameter2=$11E0
Parameter3=$000F
Parameter4=$05D0
Parameter5=$3A95
Parameter6=$E1F7
Parameter7=$0BD0
Parameter8=$1D93
Parameter9=$0895
Parameter10=$C59A
Parameter11=$08F0
Parameter12=$C598
Parameter13=$0FD0
Parameter14=$C79A
Parameter15=$0DD0
Parameter16=$C798
Parameter17=$0BD0
Parameter18=$0895
Parameter19=$BD98
Parameter20=$08D0
Parameter21=$C79A
Parameter22=$B59B
Parameter23=$10E0
Parameter24=$04D0
Parameter25=$C798
Parameter26=$02D0
Parameter27=$BD9A
Parameter28=$0895
Parameter29=$88EE
Parameter30=$93E0
Parameter31=$0197

Parameter32=$F1F7
Parameter33=$0895
Zeile0=(Wert/Adr -- ACK)
Zeile1=
Zeile2=Ein einzelnes Byte wird an den Slave
Zeile3=gesendet; das Acknowledge-Signal
Zeile4=wird auf den Stack gelegt.

[init] ============================== 21 init
Typ=F
ParamAnzahl=3
KomAnzahl=3
Parameter0=stackinit
Parameter1=main
Parameter2=end
Zeile0=Systemwort, sollte nicht vom Anwender
Zeile1=benutzt werden (und erst recht nicht
Zeile2=verändert werden).

[initCom] ======================= 22 initCom
Typ=A
ParamAnzahl=8
KomAnzahl=5
Parameter0=$549A
Parameter1=$539A
Parameter2=$09E1
Parameter3=$09B9
Parameter4=$14E6
Parameter5=$1A95
Parameter6=$F1F7
Parameter7=$0895
Zeile0=(--)
Zeile1=
Zeile2=Initialisiert die COM-Schnittstelle:
Zeile3=D0 = RxD
Zeile4=D1 = TxD

[initInt0] ====================== 23 initInt0
Typ=A
ParamAnzahl=16
KomAnzahl=14
Parameter0=$8A98
Parameter1=$929A
Parameter2=$1E91
Parameter3=$05B7
Parameter4=$0260

Parameter5=$1030
Parameter6=$11F4
Parameter7=$0E7F
Parameter8=$01C0
Parameter9=$0160
Parameter10=$05BF
Parameter11=$0BB7
Parameter12=$0064
Parameter13=$0BBF
Parameter14=$7894
Parameter15=$0895
Zeile0=(signaltyp --)
Zeile1=
Zeile2=Beispiel: signaltyp InitInt0
Zeile3=
Zeile4=Konfiguriert INT0 (Port D2) als
Zeile5=Interrupteingang und legt diesen auf High.
Zeile6=Je nach signaltyp-Wert lösen
Zeile7=unterschiedliche Eingangssignale
Zeile8=den Interrupt aus:
Zeile9=
Zeile10=0: fallende Flanke
Zeile11=1: steigende Flanke
Zeile12=
Zeile13=Interrupts werden generell zugelassen.

[initInt1] ====================== 24 initInt1
Typ=A
ParamAnzahl=16
KomAnzahl=4
Parameter0=$8B98
Parameter1=$939A
Parameter2=$1E91
Parameter3=$05B7
Parameter4=$0860
Parameter5=$1030
Parameter6=$11F4
Parameter7=$0B7F
Parameter8=$01C0
Parameter9=$0460
Parameter10=$05BF
Parameter11=$0BB7
Parameter12=$0068
Parameter13=$0BBF
Parameter14=$7894
Parameter15=$0895

Zeile0=(signaltyp --)
Zeile1=
Zeile2=Wie InitInt0, jedoch für den
Zeile3=Eingang INT1 (Port D3)

[inPortB] ======================== 25 inPortB
Typ=A
ParamAnzahl=19
KomAnzahl=8
Parameter0=$1E91
Parameter1=$28B3
Parameter2=$07E0
Parameter3=$1023
Parameter4=$01E0
Parameter5=$1030
Parameter6=$19F0
Parameter7=$000F
Parameter8=$1A95
Parameter9=$FBCF
Parameter10=$202B
Parameter11=$28BB
Parameter12=$26B3
Parameter13=$2023
Parameter14=$20E0
Parameter15=$09F0
Parameter16=$21E0
Parameter17=$2D93
Parameter18=$0895
Zeile0=(bit -- flag)
Zeile1=
Zeile2=Beispiel: bit IN_B
Zeile3=Liest den Eingang bit des Ports B und
Zeile4=legt 1/0 auf den Stack, wenn er
Zeile5=High/Low ist.
Zeile6=
Zeile7=s. a. DDRB

[loop] ============================== 26 loop
Typ=A
ParamAnzahl=17
KomAnzahl=3
Parameter0=$4F91
Parameter1=$5F91
Parameter2=$2F91
Parameter3=$3F91
Parameter4=$FF91

Parameter5=$EF91
Parameter6=$2317
Parameter7=$31F0
Parameter8=$EF93
Parameter9=$FF93
Parameter10=$2395
Parameter11=$3F93
Parameter12=$2F93
Parameter13=$0994
Parameter14=$5F93
Parameter15=$4F93
Parameter16=$0895
Zeile0=(--)
Zeile1=
Zeile2=s. a. DO

[main] ============================= 27 main
Typ=F
ParamAnzahl=9
KomAnzahl=0
Parameter0=2
Parameter1=.
Parameter2=10
Parameter3=1
Parameter4=do
Parameter5=toggleB
Parameter6=1
Parameter7=wait
Parameter8=loop

[or] ================================= 28 or
Typ=A
ParamAnzahl=5
KomAnzahl=3
Parameter0=$0E91
Parameter1=$1E91
Parameter2=$012B
Parameter3=$0D93
Parameter4=$0895
Zeile0=(a b -- erg)
Zeile1=
Zeile2=erg = a or b

[outPortB] ====================== 29 outPortB
Typ=A
ParamAnzahl=20
KomAnzahl=8
Parameter0=$3E91
Parameter1=$1E91
Parameter2=$28B3
Parameter3=$07E0
Parameter4=$1023
Parameter5=$01E0
Parameter6=$1030
Parameter7=$19F0
Parameter8=$000F
Parameter9=$1A95
Parameter10=$FBCF
Parameter11=$3030
Parameter12=$11F0
Parameter13=$202B
Parameter14=$03C0
Parameter15=$0095
Parameter16=$2023
Parameter17=$00C0
Parameter18=$28BB
Parameter19=$0895
Zeile0=(bit flag --)
Zeile1=
Zeile2=Beispiel: bit flag outPortB
Zeile3=
Zeile4=Setzt den Ausgang bit des Ports B auf
Zeile5=High/Low, wenn flag = 1/0 ist.
Zeile6=
Zeile7=s. a. DDRB

[popreg] ========================== 30 popreg
Typ=A
ParamAnzahl=15
KomAnzahl=6
Parameter0=$022D
Parameter1=$132D
Parameter2=$242D
Parameter3=$352D
Parameter4=$462D
Parameter5=$572D
Parameter6=$682D
Parameter7=$792D
Parameter8=$8A2D

Parameter9=$9B2D
Parameter10=$AC2D
Parameter11=$BD2D
Parameter12=$CE2D
Parameter13=$DF2D
Parameter14=$0895
Zeile0=(--)
Zeile1=
Zeile2=Sämtliche internen Register r16-r29
Zeile3=werden wiederhergestellt.
Zeile4=
Zeile5=s. a. INT0

[pushreg] ======================== 31 pushreg
Typ=A
ParamAnzahl=15
KomAnzahl=4
Parameter0=$202E
Parameter1=$312E
Parameter2=$422E
Parameter3=$532E
Parameter4=$642E
Parameter5=$752E
Parameter6=$862E
Parameter7=$972E
Parameter8=$A82E
Parameter9=$B92E
Parameter10=$CA2E
Parameter11=$DB2E
Parameter12=$EC2E
Parameter13=$FD2E
Parameter14=$0895
Zeile0=(--)
Zeile1=
Zeile2=Sämtliche internen Register r16-r29
Zeile3=werden gesichert (in r2-r15).

[reti] ============================ 32 reti
Typ=A
ParamAnzahl=1
KomAnzahl=5
Parameter0=$1895
Zeile0=(--)
Zeile1=
Zeile2=Interrupts werden freigegeben.
Zeile3=

Zeile4=s. a. INT0

[rot] ================================= 33 rot
Typ=A
ParamAnzahl=7
KomAnzahl=4
Parameter0=$0E91
Parameter1=$1E91
Parameter2=$2E91
Parameter3=$1D93
Parameter4=$0D93
Parameter5=$2D93
Parameter6=$0895
Zeile0=(a b c -- b c a)
Zeile1=
Zeile2=Rotiert die obersten drei Zahlen des
Zeile3=Stacks

[sei] ================================= 34 sei
Typ=A
ParamAnzahl=1
KomAnzahl=1
Parameter0=$1895
Zeile0=nötig?

[setOSCCAL] ===================== 35 setOSCCAL
Typ=A
ParamAnzahl=3
KomAnzahl=3
Parameter0=$0E91
Parameter1=$01BF
Parameter2=$0895
Zeile0=(OSCCAL --)
Zeile1=
Zeile2=Setzt den OSCCAL-Wert

[skipIF] ========================== 36 skipIF
Typ=A
ParamAnzahl=11
KomAnzahl=4
Parameter0=$11E0
Parameter1=$0E91
Parameter2=$0117
Parameter3=$09F0
Parameter4=$05C0
Parameter5=$FF91

Parameter6=$EF91
Parameter7=$E395
Parameter8=$EF93
Parameter9=$FF93
Parameter10=$0895
Zeile0=(flag --)
Zeile1=
Zeile2=Überspringt den nächsten Befehl,
Zeile3=wenn TOS gleich 1 (TRUE) ist.

[stackInit] ===================== 37 stackInit
Typ=A
ParamAnzahl=3
KomAnzahl=2
Parameter0=$A0E6
Parameter1=$B0E0
Parameter2=$0895
Zeile0=Systemwort, darf weder verändert noch
Zeile1=entfernt werden

[swap] ============================= 38 swap
Typ=A
ParamAnzahl=5
KomAnzahl=4
Parameter0=$0E91
Parameter1=$1E91
Parameter2=$0D93
Parameter3=$1D93
Parameter4=$0895
Zeile0=(a b -- b a)
Zeile1=
Zeile2=Vertauscht die beiden obersten Zahlen
Zeile3=des Stacks

[>com] ============================ 39 >com
Typ=A
ParamAnzahl=5
KomAnzahl=5
Parameter0=$0E91
Parameter1=$5D9B
Parameter2=$FDCF
Parameter3=$0CB9
Parameter4=$0895
Zeile0=(n --)
Zeile1=
Zeile2=Sendet n an die COM-Schnittstelle.

Zeile3=Vorher muss die COM-Schnittstelle mit
Zeile4=INITCOM initialisiert worden sein.

[>eprom] =========================== 40 >eprom
Typ=A
ParamAnzahl=11
KomAnzahl=4
Parameter0=$0E91
Parameter1=$1E91
Parameter2=$0F37
Parameter3=$30F4
Parameter4=$E199
Parameter5=$FECF
Parameter6=$0EBB
Parameter7=$1DBB
Parameter8=$E29A
Parameter9=$E19A
Parameter10=$0895
Zeile0=(w a --)
Zeile1=
Zeile2=Schreibt den Wert w in die Adresse a des
Zeile3=EEPROMs

[until] ============================ 41 until
Typ=A
ParamAnzahl=14
KomAnzahl=3
Parameter0=$4F91
Parameter1=$5F91
Parameter2=$FF91
Parameter3=$EF91
Parameter4=$20E0
Parameter5=$3E91
Parameter6=$2317
Parameter7=$19F4
Parameter8=$EF93
Parameter9=$FF93
Parameter10=$0994
Parameter11=$5F93
Parameter12=$4F93
Parameter13=$0895
Zeile0=(n --)
Zeile1=
Zeile2=s. BEGIN

[wait] ============================= 42 wait
Typ=F
ParamAnzahl=11
KomAnzahl=3
Parameter0=1
Parameter1=do
Parameter2=250
Parameter3=250
Parameter4=250
Parameter5=250
Parameter6=waitms
Parameter7=waitms
Parameter8=waitms
Parameter9=waitms
Parameter10=loop
Zeile0=(s --)
Zeile1=
Zeile2=Wartet s Sekunden

[wait1ms] ======================== 43 wait1ms
Typ=A
ParamAnzahl=5
KomAnzahl=3
Parameter0=$88EE
Parameter1=$93E0
Parameter2=$0197
Parameter3=$F1F7
Parameter4=$0895
Zeile0=(--)
Zeile1=
Zeile2=Wartet 1 Millisekunde

[waitms] =========================== 44 waitms
Typ=F
ParamAnzahl=4
KomAnzahl=3
Parameter0=1
Parameter1=do
Parameter2=wait1ms
Parameter3=loop
Zeile0=(n --)
Zeile1=
Zeile2=Wartet n Millisekunden

[wdogOff] ======================== 45 wdogOff
Typ=A

ParamAnzahl=6
KomAnzahl=3
Parameter0=$A895
Parameter1=$08E1
Parameter2=$01BD
Parameter3=$00E0
Parameter4=$01BD
Parameter5=$0895
Zeile0=(--)
Zeile1=
Zeile2=Schaltet den Watchdog aus

[xor] =============================== 46 xor
Typ=A
ParamAnzahl=5
KomAnzahl=3
Parameter0=$0E91
Parameter1=$1E91
Parameter2=$0127
Parameter3=$0D93
Parameter4=$0895
Zeile0=(a b -- erg)
Zeile1=
Zeile2=erg = a xor b

[int0] ============================= 47 int0
Typ=F
ParamAnzahl=0
KomAnzahl=12
Zeile0=Dieses Wort wird aufgerufen, wenn
Zeile1=das INT0-Interrupt ausgelöst wird,
Zeile2=muss vom Anwender überschrieben
Zeile3=werden.
Zeile4=
Zeile5=Aufbau eines Interruptwortes:
Zeile6=
Zeile7=: INT0 pushreg ... <beliebige Wörter>
Zeile8=... popreg reti;
Zeile9=
Zeile10=Während das Wort INT0 ausgeführt wird,
Zeile11=sind sämtliche Interrupts gesperrt.

[int1] ============================= 48 int1
Typ=F
ParamAnzahl=0
KomAnzahl=4
Zeile0=s. INT0
Zeile1=
Zeile2=Muss vom Anwender überschrieben
Zeile3=werden.

[-] ================================== 49 -
Typ=A
ParamAnzahl=5
KomAnzahl=3
Parameter0=$1E91
Parameter1=$0E91
Parameter2=$011B
Parameter3=$0D93
Parameter4=$0895
Zeile0=(a b -- erg)
Zeile1=
Zeile2=erg = a – b

[*] ================================== 50 *
Typ=F
ParamAnzahl=9
KomAnzahl=3
Parameter0=0
Parameter1=SWAP
Parameter2=1
Parameter3=DO
Parameter4=SWAP
Parameter5=DUP
Parameter6=ROT
Parameter7=+
Parameter8=LOOP
Zeile0=(a b -- erg)
Zeile1=
Zeile2=erg = a*b

[DDRB] ============================= 51 DDRB
Typ=A
ParamAnzahl=3
KomAnzahl=4
Parameter0=$0E91
Parameter1=$07BB
Parameter2=$0895

Zeile0=(r --)
Zeile1=
Zeile2=Schreibt r in das Datenrichtungsregister
Zeile3=von Port B

[over] ============================ 52 over
Typ=A
ParamAnzahl=6
KomAnzahl=4
Parameter0=$1E91
Parameter1=$0E91
Parameter2=$0D93
Parameter3=$1D93
Parameter4=$0D93
Parameter5=$0895
Zeile0=(a b -- a b a)
Zeile1=
Zeile2=Kopiert das zweitoberste Element des
Zeile3=Stacks auf den TOS

[>R] ================================= 53 >R
Typ=A
ParamAnzahl=7
KomAnzahl=3
Parameter0=$2F91
Parameter1=$1F91
Parameter2=$0E91
Parameter3=$0F93
Parameter4=$1F93
Parameter5=$2F93
Parameter6=$0895
Zeile0=(n --)
Zeile1=
Zeile2=schiebt TOS auf den Returnstack

[R>] ================================= 54 R>
Typ=A
ParamAnzahl=7
KomAnzahl=4
Parameter0=$2F91
Parameter1=$1F91
Parameter2=$0F91
Parameter3=$0D93
Parameter4=$1F93
Parameter5=$2F93
Parameter6=$0895

Zeile0=(-- x)
Zeile1=
Zeile2=holt Zahl vom Returnstack und legt sie
Zeile3=auf den (Arbeits-) Stack

[T0?] ============================= 55 T0?
Typ=F
ParamAnzahl=8
KomAnzahl=6
Parameter0=2
Parameter1=0
Parameter2=ddBitD
Parameter3=2
Parameter4=1
Parameter5=outPortD
Parameter6=2
Parameter7=InPortD
Zeile0=(-- bit)
Zeile1=
Zeile2=Legt 1/0 auf Stack, wenn Taster T0
Zeile3=offen/geschlossen (D2=1/0)
Zeile4=
Zeile5=PortD.2 wird automatisch konfiguriert.

[T1?] ============================= 56 T1?
Typ=F
ParamAnzahl=8
KomAnzahl=6
Parameter0=3
Parameter1=0
Parameter2=ddBitD
Parameter3=3
Parameter4=1
Parameter5=outPortD
Parameter6=3
Parameter7=InPortD
Zeile0=(-- bit)
Zeile1=
Zeile2=Legt 1/0 auf Stack, wenn Taster T1
Zeile3=offen/geschlossen (D3=1/0)
Zeile4=
Zeile5=PortD.3 wird automatisch konfiguriert.

[DDBitD] ========================= 57 DDRBitD
Typ=A
ParamAnzahl=19
KomAnzahl=5
Parameter0=$3E91
Parameter1=$1E91
Parameter2=$21B3
Parameter3=$07E0
Parameter4=$1023
Parameter5=$01E0
Parameter6=$1030
Parameter7=$19F0
Parameter8=$000F
Parameter9=$1A95
Parameter10=$FBCF
Parameter11=$3030
Parameter12=$11F0
Parameter13=$202B
Parameter14=$02C0
Parameter15=$0095
Parameter16=$2023
Parameter17=$21BB
Parameter18=$0895
Zeile0=(bit flag --)
Zeile1=
Zeile2=bit flag DDBitB setzt den Anschluss bit
Zeile3=des Ports D als Ausgang, wenn flag = 1,
Zeile4=sonst als Eingang

[DDRD] ============================== 58 DDRD
Typ=A
ParamAnzahl=3
KomAnzahl=4
Parameter0=$0E91
Parameter1=$01BB
Parameter2=$0895
Zeile0=(d --)
Zeile1=
Zeile2=schreibt d in das Datenrichtungsregister
Zeile3=des Ports D.

[InPortD] ======================= 59 InPortD
Typ=A
ParamAnzahl=19
KomAnzahl=9
Parameter0=$1E91

Parameter1=$22B3
Parameter2=$07E0
Parameter3=$1023
Parameter4=$01E0
Parameter5=$1030
Parameter6=$19F0
Parameter7=$000F
Parameter8=$1A95
Parameter9=$FBCF
Parameter10=$202B
Parameter11=$22BB
Parameter12=$20B3
Parameter13=$2023
Parameter14=$20E0
Parameter15=$09F0
Parameter16=$21E0
Parameter17=$2D93
Parameter18=$0895
Zeile0=(bit -- flag)
Zeile1=
Zeile2=bit InPortD
Zeile3=
Zeile4=liest den Eingang bit des Ports D und
Zeile5=legt 1/0 auf den Stack, wenn er
Zeile6=high/low ist
Zeile7=
Zeile8=Vgl. DDRD und DDBitD

[/] ==================================== 60 /
Typ=A
ParamAnzahl=11
KomAnzahl=4
Parameter0=$1E91
Parameter1=$0E91
Parameter2=$40E0
Parameter3=$0117
Parameter4=$18F4
Parameter5=$4D93
Parameter6=$0D93
Parameter7=$0895
Parameter8=$011B
Parameter9=$4395
Parameter10=$F8CF
Zeile0=(a b -- erg rest)
Zeile1=
Zeile2=dividiert a durch b; der Rest der

Zeile3=ganzzahligen Division steht in "rest".

[outPortD] ====================== 61 outPortD
Typ=A
ParamAnzahl=19
KomAnzahl=8
Parameter0=$3E91
Parameter1=$1E91
Parameter2=$22B3
Parameter3=$07E0
Parameter4=$1023
Parameter5=$01E0
Parameter6=$1030
Parameter7=$19F0
Parameter8=$000F
Parameter9=$1A95
Parameter10=$FBCF
Parameter11=$3030
Parameter12=$11F0
Parameter13=$202B
Parameter14=$02C0
Parameter15=$0095
Parameter16=$2023
Parameter17=$22BB
Parameter18=$0895
Zeile0=(bit flag --)
Zeile1=
Zeile2=Beispiel: bit flag outPortD
Zeile3=
Zeile4=Setzt den Ausgang bit des Ports D auf
Zeile5=High/Low, wenn flag = 1/0 ist.
Zeile6=
Zeile7=s. a. DDRD

[not] ================================ 62 not
Typ=F
ParamAnzahl=2
KomAnzahl=3
Parameter0=0
Parameter1=equal
Zeile0=(flag -- flag)
Zeile1=
Zeile2=negiert einen Wahrheitswert (1/0).

[t1Capt] =========================== 63 t1Capt
Typ=F
ParamAnzahl=0
KomAnzahl=13
Zeile0=Dieses Wort wird aufgerufen, wenn
Zeile1=das Timer/Counter1-Capture-Event-
Zeile2=Interrupt ausgelöst wird,
Zeile3=muss vom Anwender überschrieben
Zeile4=werden.
Zeile5=
Zeile6=Aufbau eines Interruptwortes (INT0):
Zeile7=
Zeile8=: INT0 pushreg ... <beliebige Wörter>
Zeile9=... popreg reti;
Zeile10=
Zeile11=Während das Wort INT0 ausgeführt wird,
Zeile12=sind sämtliche Interrupts gesperrt.

[t1CompA] ======================== 64 t1CompA
Typ=F
ParamAnzahl=0
KomAnzahl=13
Zeile0=Dieses Wort wird aufgerufen, wenn
Zeile1=das Timer/Counter1-Compare-Match-A-
Zeile2=Interrupt ausgelöst wird,
Zeile3=muss vom Anwender überschrieben
Zeile4=werden.
Zeile5=
Zeile6=Aufbau eines Interruptwortes (INT0):
Zeile7=
Zeile8=: INT0 pushreg ... <beliebige Wörter>
Zeile9=... popreg reti;
Zeile10=
Zeile11=Während das Wort INT0 ausgeführt wird,
Zeile12=sind sämtliche Interrupts gesperrt.

[t1Ovf] =========================== 65 t1Ovf
Typ=F
ParamAnzahl=0
KomAnzahl=13
Zeile0=Dieses Wort wird aufgerufen, wenn
Zeile1=das Timer/Counter1-Overflow-Interrupt
Zeile2=ausgelöst wird,
Zeile3=muss vom Anwender überschrieben
Zeile4=werden.
Zeile5=

Zeile6=Aufbau eines Interruptwortes (INT0):
Zeile7=
Zeile8=: INT0 pushreg ... <beliebige Wörter>
Zeile9=... popreg reti;
Zeile10=
Zeile11=Während das Wort INT0 ausgeführt wird,
Zeile12=sind sämtliche Interrupts gesperrt.

[t0Ovf] ============================ 66 t0Ovf
Typ=F
ParamAnzahl=0
KomAnzahl=13
Zeile0=Dieses Wort wird aufgerufen, wenn
Zeile1=das Timer/Counter0-Overflow-Interrupt
Zeile2=ausgelöst wird,
Zeile3=muss vom Anwender überschrieben
Zeile4=werden.
Zeile5=
Zeile6=Aufbau eines Interruptwortes (INT0):
Zeile7=
Zeile8=: INT0 pushreg ... <beliebige Wörter>
Zeile9=... popreg reti;
Zeile10=
Zeile11=Während das Wort INT0 ausgeführt wird,
Zeile12=sind sämtliche Interrupts gesperrt.

[usart0Rx] ===================== 67 usart0Rx
Typ=F
ParamAnzahl=0
KomAnzahl=13
Zeile0=Dieses Wort wird aufgerufen, wenn
Zeile1=das USART0-RX-Complete-Interrupt
Zeile2=ausgelöst wird,
Zeile3=muss vom Anwender überschrieben
Zeile4=werden.
Zeile5=
Zeile6=Aufbau eines Interruptwortes (INT0):
Zeile7=
Zeile8=: INT0 pushreg ... <beliebige Wörter>
Zeile9=... popreg reti;
Zeile10=
Zeile11=Während das Wort INT0 ausgeführt wird,
Zeile12=sind sämtliche Interrupts gesperrt.

[usart0Udre] ================== 68 usart0Udre
Typ=F
ParamAnzahl=0
KomAnzahl=13
Zeile0=Dieses Wort wird aufgerufen, wenn
Zeile1=das USART0-Data-Register-Empty-
Zeile2=Interrupt ausgelöst wird,
Zeile3=muss vom Anwender überschrieben
Zeile4=werden.
Zeile5=
Zeile6=Aufbau eines Interruptwortes (INT0):
Zeile7=
Zeile8=: INT0 pushreg ... <beliebige Wörter>
Zeile9=... popreg reti;
Zeile10=
Zeile11=Während das Wort INT0 ausgeführt wird,
Zeile12=sind sämtliche Interrupts gesperrt.

[usart0Tx] ====================== 69 usart0Tx
Typ=F
ParamAnzahl=0
KomAnzahl=13
Zeile0=Dieses Wort wird aufgerufen, wenn
Zeile1=das USART0-TX-Complete-Interrupt
Zeile2=ausgelöst wird,
Zeile3=muss vom Anwender überschrieben
Zeile4=werden.
Zeile5=
Zeile6=Aufbau eines Interruptwortes (INT0):
Zeile7=
Zeile8=: INT0 pushreg ... <beliebige Wörter>
Zeile9=... popreg reti;
Zeile10=
Zeile11=Während das Wort INT0 ausgeführt wird,
Zeile12=sind sämtliche Interrupts gesperrt.

[analogComp] ================== 70 analogComp
Typ=F
ParamAnzahl=0
KomAnzahl=13
Zeile0=Dieses Wort wird aufgerufen, wenn
Zeile1=das Analog-Comparator-Interrupt
Zeile2=ausgelöst wird,
Zeile3=muss vom Anwender überschrieben
Zeile4=werden.
Zeile5=

Zeile6=Aufbau eines Interruptwortes (INT0):
Zeile7=
Zeile8=: INT0 pushreg ... <beliebige Wörter>
Zeile9=... popreg reti;
Zeile10=
Zeile11=Während das Wort INT0 ausgeführt wird,
Zeile12=sind sämtliche Interrupts gesperrt.

[pCInt] ============================ 71 pCInt
Typ=F
ParamAnzahl=0
KomAnzahl=12
Zeile0=Dieses Wort wird aufgerufen, wenn
Zeile1=das Pin-Change-Interrupt ausgelöst wird,
Zeile2=muss vom Anwender überschrieben
Zeile3=werden.
Zeile4=
Zeile5=Aufbau eines Interruptwortes (INT0):
Zeile6=
Zeile7=: INT0 pushreg ... <beliebige Wörter>
Zeile8=... popreg reti;
Zeile9=
Zeile10=Während das Wort INT0 ausgeführt wird,
Zeile11=sind sämtliche Interrupts gesperrt.

[t1CompB] ======================== 72 t1CompB
Typ=F
ParamAnzahl=0
KomAnzahl=13
Zeile0=Dieses Wort wird aufgerufen, wenn
Zeile1=das Timer/Counter1-Compare-Match-B-
Zeile2=Interrupt ausgelöst wird,
Zeile3=muss vom Anwender überschrieben
Zeile4=werden.
Zeile5=
Zeile6=Aufbau eines Interruptwortes (INT0):
Zeile7=
Zeile8=: INT0 pushreg ... <beliebige Wörter>
Zeile9=... popreg reti;
Zeile10=
Zeile11=Während das Wort INT0 ausgeführt wird,
Zeile12=sind sämtliche Interrupts gesperrt.

[t0CompA] ======================== 73 t0CompA
Typ=F
ParamAnzahl=0
KomAnzahl=13
Zeile0=Dieses Wort wird aufgerufen, wenn
Zeile1=das Timer/Counter0-Compare-Match-A-
Zeile2=Interrupt ausgelöst wird,
Zeile3=muss vom Anwender überschrieben
Zeile4=werden.
Zeile5=
Zeile6=Aufbau eines Interruptwortes (INT0):
Zeile7=
Zeile8=: INT0 pushreg ... <beliebige Wörter>
Zeile9=... popreg reti;
Zeile10=
Zeile11=Während das Wort INT0 ausgeführt wird,
Zeile12=sind sämtliche Interrupts gesperrt.

[t0CompB] ======================== 74 t0CompB
Typ=F
ParamAnzahl=0
KomAnzahl=13
Zeile0=Dieses Wort wird aufgerufen, wenn
Zeile1=das Timer/Counter0-Compare-Match-B-
Zeile2=Interrupt ausgelöst wird,
Zeile3=muss vom Anwender überschrieben
Zeile4=werden.
Zeile5=
Zeile6=Aufbau eines Interruptwortes (INT0):
Zeile7=
Zeile8=: INT0 pushreg ... <beliebige Wörter>
Zeile9=... popreg reti;
Zeile10=
Zeile11=Während das Wort INT0 ausgeführt wird,
Zeile12=sind sämtliche Interrupts gesperrt.

[usiStart] ===================== 75 usiStart
Typ=F
ParamAnzahl=5
KomAnzahl=0
Parameter0=pushreg
Parameter1=1
Parameter2=.
Parameter3=popreg
Parameter4=reti

[usiOvf] ========================== 76 usiOvf
Typ=F
ParamAnzahl=0
KomAnzahl=12
Zeile0=Dieses Wort wird aufgerufen, wenn
Zeile1=das USI-Overflow-Interrupt ausgelöst wird,
Zeile2=muss vom Anwender überschrieben
Zeile3=werden.
Zeile4=
Zeile5=Aufbau eines Interruptwortes (INT0):
Zeile6=
Zeile7=: INT0 pushreg ... <beliebige Wörter>
Zeile8=... popreg reti;
Zeile9=
Zeile10=Während das Wort INT0 ausgeführt wird,
Zeile11=sind sämtliche Interrupts gesperrt.

[eeReady] ========================= 77 eeReady
Typ=F
ParamAnzahl=0
KomAnzahl=13
Zeile0=Dieses Wort wird aufgerufen, wenn
Zeile1=das EEPROM-Ready-Interrupt
Zeile2=ausgelöst wird,
Zeile3=muss vom Anwender überschrieben
Zeile4=werden.
Zeile5=
Zeile6=Aufbau eines Interruptwortes (INT0):
Zeile7=
Zeile8=: INT0 pushreg ... <beliebige Wörter>
Zeile9=... popreg reti;
Zeile10=
Zeile11=Während das Wort INT0 ausgeführt wird,
Zeile12=sind sämtliche Interrupts gesperrt.

[wdtOvf] ========================== 78 wdtOvf
Typ=F
ParamAnzahl=0
KomAnzahl=13
Zeile0=Dieses Wort wird aufgerufen, wenn
Zeile1=das Watchdog-Timer-Overflow-Interrupt
Zeile2=ausgelöst wird,
Zeile3=muss vom Anwender überschrieben
Zeile4=werden.
Zeile5=
Zeile6=Aufbau eines Interruptwortes (INT0):

Zeile7=
Zeile8=: INT0 pushreg ... <beliebige Wörter>
Zeile9=... popreg reti;
Zeile10=
Zeile11=Während das Wort INT0 ausgeführt wird,
Zeile12=sind sämtliche Interrupts gesperrt.

[>sram] =========================== 79 >sram
Typ=A
ParamAnzahl=5
KomAnzahl=4
Parameter0=$CE91
Parameter1=$D0E0
Parameter2=$1E91
Parameter3=$1883
Parameter4=$0895
Zeile0=(w a --)
Zeile1=
Zeile2=schreibt den Wert w in das SRAM-Register
Zeile3=mit der Adresse a

[sram>] =========================== 80 sram>]
Typ=A
ParamAnzahl=5
KomAnzahl=5
Parameter0=$CE91
Parameter1=$D0E0
Parameter2=$1881
Parameter3=$1D93
Parameter4=$0895
Zeile0=(a -- w)
Zeile1=
Zeile2=legt den Wert w aus dem SRAM-
Zeile3=Register mit der Adresse a auf den
Zeile4=Stack.

[toggleB] ======================= 81 toggleB
Typ=A
ParamAnzahl=4
KomAnzahl=4
Parameter0=$08B3
Parameter1=$0095
Parameter2=$08BB
Parameter3=$0895
Zeile0=(--)
Zeile1=

Zeile2=toggelt Port B, d. h. es wird
Zeile3=das Einerkomplement gebildet.

[initt0ovf] ==================== 82 initt0ovf
Typ=A
ParamAnzahl=11
KomAnzahl=19
Parameter0=$1E91
Parameter1=$0E91
Parameter2=$12BF
Parameter3=$0770
Parameter4=$03BF
Parameter5=$20E0
Parameter6=$39B7
Parameter7=$3260
Parameter8=$39BF
Parameter9=$7894
Parameter10=$0895
Zeile0=(typ preset --)
Zeile1=
Zeile2=Initialisiert den Timer0-Interrupt:
Zeile3=
Zeile4=typ
Zeile5=0: Timer stoppen/deaktivieren
Zeile6=1: Systemtakt/1
Zeile7=2: Systemtakt/8
Zeile8=3: Systemtakt/64
Zeile9=4: Systemtakt/256
Zeile10=5: Systemtakt/1024
Zeile11=6: ext. Takt, fallend an T0
Zeile12=7: ext. Takt, steigend an T0
Zeile13=
Zeile14=Timer-Interrupt freigegeben
Zeile15=alle Interrupts freigegeben
Zeile16=
Zeile17=presetwert muss in Interruptroutine
Zeile18=immer wieder neu gesetzt werden.

[setTimer0] ==================== 83 setTimer0
Typ=A
ParamAnzahl=3
KomAnzahl=5
Parameter0=$1E91
Parameter1=$12BF
Parameter2=$0895
Zeile0=(preset --)

Zeile1=
Zeile2=lädt den Wert preset in das Zählregister
Zeile3=des Timers 0.
Zeile4=

END ==

GEORG HEINRICHS
ÜBER MICH

Geboren in Kempen
Abitur am Gymnasium Thomaeum in Kempen
Studium der Mathematik und Physik in Bonn, 1. Staatsexamen
Ableisten der Wehrpflicht in Porz bei Köln
Diplom in Mathematik

Referendar am Studienseminar in Krefeld, 2. Staatsexamen
Lehrer am Franz-Meyers-Gymnasium in Mönchengladbach
Fachmoderator für Informatik (SI) bei der Bezirksregierung Düsseldorf
Fachmoderator für Strahlenschutz bei der Bezirksregierung Düsseldorf
Fachmoderator für Physik beim KT Mönchengladbach

Publikationen zu verschiedenen Themen der Physik und Informatik

Pensioniert

Verheiratet, drei Kinder
Interessen: Kammermusik, Lesen, Computer, alte Sprachen, Reisen,
Ausflüge mit dem Fahrrad

http://www.g-heinrichs.de/wordpress/index.php/attiny/
http://www.g-heinrichs.de/wordpress/index.php/ueber-mich/

GEORG HEINRICHS

ABOUT ME

Born in Kempen/Germany
High school graduation at the Gymnasium Thomaeum in Kempen
Study of maths and physics in Bonn, 1st state exam
Military service at Porz near Cologne
Diploma in Mathematics

Trainee at the study seminar in Krefeld, and 2nd state exam
Teacher at Franz-Meyers-Gymnasium in Mönchengladbach
Specialist Moderator for Informatics at school in (SI) in Düsseldorf
Specialist for Radiation Protection at school in Dusseldorf
Fachmoderator for physics at KT Mönchengladbach

Publications on various topics of physics and computer science

Now retired
Married, three children

Interests: chamber music, reading, computer, old languages, travelling, bike rides

http://www.g-heinrichs.de/wordpress/index.php/attiny/
http://www.g-heinrichs.de/wordpress/index.php/ueber-mich/